DIALOGUES CONCERNING THE FOUNDATIONS OF ETHICS

Dialogues Concerning the Foundations of Ethics

K. Richard Garrett

Rowman & Littlefield Publishers, Inc.

ROWMAN & LITTLEFIELD PUBLISHERS, INC.

Published in the United States of America
by Rowman & Littlefield Publishers, Inc.
8705 Bollman Place, Savage, Maryland 20763

British Cataloging in Publication Information Available

Library of Congress Cataloging-in-Publication Data

Garrett, K. Richard.
  Dialogues concerning the foundations of ethics /
K. Richard Garrett.
    p.   cm.
    1. Ethics.   2. Ethical relativism.   I. Title.
BJ1012.G37   1990   171—dc20   90–9070 CIP

ISBN 0–8476–7639–0 (cloth : alk. paper)
ISBN 0–8476–7640–4 (pbk. : alk. paper)

5   4   3   2   1

Printed in the United States of America

 ᵀᴹ The paper used in this publication meets the minimum requirements of
American National Standard for Information Sciences—Permanence of
Paper for Printed Library Materials, ANSI Z39.48–1984.

Contents

Part III Homer's Case for Ethical Relativism   35

Part IV Siddhartha's Absolutist Position Stated   59

Part V Dilemma's and Max's Attacks on Siddhartha's Views   75

Introduction

These dialogues explore the rational basis for moral judgment from both the perspective of moral relativism as well as that of moral absolutism. The intent is to state the main features of the relativist-absolutist debate over the foundations of ethics in a clear and interesting fashion that presupposes no prior knowledge of philosophy. The participants include three relativists: Dilemma (a social scientist), Max (a logician and philosopher), and Homer (a classics scholar). Siddhartha, an absolutist, is a retired scholar of both eastern and western philosophy. Although there are more spokesmen on behalf of relativism than on behalf of absolutism, each relativist offers a progressively richer variety of relativism, which is increasingly closer to absolutism, until a certain philosophic pride of place is granted absolutism at the end of the dialogues. Throughout, the aim is to arouse an awareness of the issues involved in the debate rather than give definitive answers, and, although absolutism is favored, no final resolution of the debate is attempted.

Part I

Dilemma's Case for Ethical Relativism

Max: Homer, it is good to see you. You are just in time. Dilemma and I were just about to enter into another debate with our guest, Siddhartha, over the issue of relativism versus absolutism. Having seen Siddhartha in action the other night, I think we can use all the reinforcements we can get.

Homer: What set you off this time?

Max: Dilemma was telling Siddhartha about the Ikes who, when faced with extreme conditions of starvation, abandoned all of their normal patterns of interaction. He deliberately drew Siddhartha into the discussion by describing some of the horrible things that went on during the Ikes' last days.

Homer: I must confess I don't know who the Ikes are.

Max: "Were" would be putting it more accurately, Homer. The last of the Ikes died more than a decade ago.

Homer: I see. Well, then, who were they?

Max: They were an African tribe who, at one time, lived off the land by hunting. The African government forced them to abandon their hunting grounds and live in a much smaller area. The plan was that they would become farmers instead of hunters.

But tragically, the Ikes could not adjust to the domestic rigors of farm life, and, eventually, they all died of starvation.

Homer: And how did stories about the Ikes lead into a discussion of moral relativism and moral absolutism?

Dilemma: I was telling Siddhartha about an anthropologist who was studying the Ikes during the later days of their civilization. The anthropologist mentioned numerous horrible incidents that took place.

Homer: Such as what?

Dilemma: In one case, a son stole food from his sick father until the old man finally died of starvation. In another case, two parents sent their three-year-old daughter out into the forest so that they would not have to feed her. When she kept returning after repeated attempts to get rid of her, the parents finally sealed her in a mud hut and left her there to die. At first the anthropologist was horrified by such incidents and condemned the Ikes for their callous actions. But as time went by, he had only sympathy for them. He concluded that he could not judge them by his standards, that, as other anthropologists before him had done after studying people of another culture, he could only judge them by their own standards, if at all. When I told Siddhartha I agreed with the anthropologist, Siddhartha took exception, as I anticipated he would.

Siddhartha: Yes, I confess. I took Dilemma's bait. I said that although the anthropologist's sympathy for the Ikes was admirable and that I also agreed we should not judge them as human beings (for I believe we should leave that sort of thing to God), I could not entirely agree with the anthropologist's attitude.

Homer: Where did you disagree?

Siddhartha: I claimed that, although we can't stand in judgment of the moral worth of the Ikes, or anyone, we can morally evaluate their *actions* and ask ourselves: Did the various people in the stories do the right thing? More importantly I argued that it is not a question of their standards vs. ours, but of what is the right thing for *anyone* to do in such situations. I believe that what would be right for anyone would be right for everyone.

Homer: I see. So, like a good moral relativist, Dilemma, you rejected the idea that there is a single, transcultural moral standard or norm by which all people's actions can be judged. Instead, you argued that we can only judge the Ikes by their own standards. Then you, Siddhartha, picked up the absolutist's banner and made the opposite claim, namely, that there is but one single morality by which the actions of the Ikes and everyone else can be judged. Is that the picture?

Max: That is it exactly. At that point, I stepped in with the suggestion that since Siddhartha will be leaving us tomorrow, it would be valuable if each of us had an opportunity to state and defend his views and that Siddhartha should have the opportunity to question and comment upon each of us and also to have the last word, since he is our guest and the only absolutist amongst us.

Homer: That sounds like a good plan to me.

Max: Good, then please join us. You are just in time because Dilemma was just about to state his views on the matter.

Homer: My pleasure. Please tell us your views, Dilemma.

Dilemma: As I see it, the only way to approach the question of morality is in a scientific way. If you want to understand some phenomenon, you have to pay your dues with plenty of observation. Theories about morality—or anything else—are worthless unless they fit the data. If the Ikes were the only exception to our moral standards, Siddhartha, I would have to agree with you and say they had gone afoul. But the facts are otherwise. Anthropologists have found equally dramatic departures from our moral values in every part of the globe. The fact is, Siddhartha, that agreement in moral values is the exception, diversity is the rule. How, in face of such facts, dare we set up our values as the moral standards for all the world?

moral diversity disproves realism (!)

Siddhartha: What do you mean by "our moral values," Dilemma?

Dilemma: I mean our Western values, the values of middle America.

Siddhartha: Then let me remind you that although I have spent half of my life in the West, I was raised in the East. As a transplanted Easterner on Western soil, I have been forced to think doubly about these questions, not simply as a professional philosopher, but more importantly as someone finding himself an adult confronted with very different moral values than I had known as a youngster. But speaking of facts, one of the facts that struck me when I came to America is how many Americas there really are. I do not find in your own country a single monolithic system of values, but a plurality of values. There are many different ethnic groups, religious groups, and classes in America, and they all have different moral values.

Dilemma: Fine. I accept your point. But that only adds support to what I said, Siddhartha, by illustrating the tremendous variety of moral values that exist in the world. How, in the face of such overwhelming diversity of moral values, can you tell me there is only one morality?

Siddhartha: There is no denying the facts, Dilemma. I wish to be as faithful to them as you do. It is not the facts that separate us. We both agree that there is an overwhelming variety of moral norms. What distinguishes us is our *interpretation* of the facts. You think it follows that because what-people-take-to-be-moral varies, what-really-is-moral varies. But that only follows if what-people-take-to-be-moral and what-really-is-moral amount to the same thing.

Dilemma: And just what is the alternative to that?

Siddhartha: I deny that what people take to be moral is necessarily the same as what really is moral. I explain the diversity of moral norms by assuming that the single universal morality is not known nor understood universally, that people are in various

[handwritten notes in top margin: "diversity about shape of earth → relativism. Why should it do so in case of moral beliefs? Errors are possible"]

stages of understanding that single morality. That, after all, is an alternative.

Dilemma: On what grounds?

Siddhartha: Consider an analogy. Suppose we were to discover a tremendous diversity among cultures regarding the shape of the earth. Some thought it was flat, some that it was shaped like an egg, still others thought it to be like a pyramid. It would scarcely follow from the fact that various cultures have different conceptions of the earth's shape that the earth actually had many shapes. For you would not say that the real shape of the earth was necessarily the same thing as what people take it to be, would you?

Dilemma: Heavens, no.

Siddhartha: A better explanation of the diversity of opinions about the shape of the earth is to assume that the various cultures had incomplete and incorrect conceptions of the earth's real shape. Do you agree?

Dilemma: Certainly.

Siddhartha: Then with respect to the shape of the earth one can also be a relativist or an absolutist, and just now you told me you would remain an absolutist about the shape of the earth no matter how much diversity you found on the topic. That is exactly my stance on the matter of morality and the reason I remain unimpressed by all of the findings of the anthropologists.

Dilemma: I can see why you consider my first argument inadequate, Siddhartha. By itself it proves nothing. But I think it, combined with a second consideration, constitutes a very powerful argument.

Siddhartha: And what is that?

Dilemma: Your reply to my first argument assumes that the analogy between the shape of the earth and morality holds, that they are the same sort of phenomenon. But I say they are not.

The shape of the earth has to do with the earth and not with culture; but morality concerns culture, for morality is a part of a culture, and the shape of the earth is not. Hence, we have a right to expect a science such as anthropology, which studies cultures, to throw light upon morality, but not upon the shape of the earth.

Siddhartha: Your point is well taken, Dilemma. So let me offer you a second analogy, one that is much closer to morality. Would you consider the practice of medicine a part of culture or not?

Dilemma: I would certainly include medicine as part of a culture.

Siddhartha: Well then, suppose that within the field of medicine itself, you discovered different approaches to treating cancer patients and various conceptions of what cancer was. Some people might conceive of cancer as a punishment by the gods, others might take it to be possession by evil spirits, and still others as the presence of viruses. Yet, suppose they are all dealing with the same thing; not all of these conceptions of cancer could be correct. Indeed, only one of these concepts could be the one that is completely adequate. Would you agree?

Dilemma: I would.

Siddhartha: So the picture we get is of a diversity of medicines with a variety of treatments for cancer—some of them quite inadequate, some helpful but crude, like removing the cancerous tissue by surgery, and some one or few, perhaps, maximally effective. Now tell me whose treatment of cancer is most likely to be effective—societies that have the best conception of what cancer is, or societies that have the most inadequate conception of what cancer is?

Dilemma: It would be reasonable to suppose that the former had the best methods of treatment, of course.

next 5 compares moral moral views with moral views on how to combat a disease, like cancer

Siddhartha: Good. Then I want you to think of immorality as the cancer of society—the disorderly and destructive behavior of its members—and morality as the healthy state of society. The various mores or moral rules of the various societies correspond to their various treatment methods of that social cancer, of which each society has a more or less adequate conception. The more adequate a society's conception of the social cancer of immorality and of the state of social health or morality, the better its treatment of that disease is likely to be. My absolutist thesis is that all societies are struggling with essentially the same societal disease and are in need of attaining the same basic state of health—that morality or social health is essentially the same for all societies in spite of the diversity of treatment used to attain moral health.

Dilemma: I can see a certain attractiveness in the model you offer, Siddhartha, but there is still one thing you are forgetting.

Siddhartha: What is that?

Dilemma: Modern medicine has made a certain progress over the years by demonstrating that medical practices and conceptions of illness can be firmly grounded in scientific research. Therefore, it is reasonable to speak of a more or less objective conception of illness and health in the field of medicine. That is, scientific medical research has demonstrated that some medical practices and some conceptions of health and illness are more adequate than others. But with respect to various moral practices and various conceptions of morality, things have turned out otherwise. Science has not been able to establish one set of moral practices or some one, or few, conceptions of morality to be superior to others. So here, I say, science points to a difference between medicine and morality.

Siddhartha: I quite agree with you, Dilemma, that medicine and morality are not exactly analogous. For while medicine has to do with a mastery of our bodies, morality concerns the mastery of the whole self and of life as a whole and is not likely to be experimentally established in the same way that medicine

S: moral argument has its own standards of proof

has been. But that does not mean there is no rational way to
decide which conception of morality is the more adequate or
even the most adequate one. There are rational procedures other
than experimentation for determining the truth of some propo-
sitions. No one has ever performed an experiment to demonstrate the Pythagorean theorem in geometry, yet no one who
has seen the proof for it would deny that it is rationally
grounded.

Dilemma: I agree. But are you suggesting that morality is like
mathematics? That an argument in ethics is like a proof in
mathematics or geometry?

Siddhartha: Not at all. I am simply suggesting that we must
keep an open mind about what constitutes a rational demonstra-
tion or argument for some truth. We must take each argument,
moral or otherwise, on its own merits and judge it accordingly.
That is all I am saying. And so it is with respect to the absolutist's claim that there is only one true morality. We must look at
the arguments presented on behalf of that claim and evaluate
them on their own merit, without some preconception of what a
good argument has to look like.

Dilemma: I will accept your point for the time being, Siddhartha, just to see where you go from here, but there is something
you are still overlooking.

Siddhartha: What is that?

Dilemma: There are good reasons to expect that morality
cannot be established rationally. For if you look at the facts as I
do, then you can't help but note that there is something very
special about moral utterances that sets them off from ordinary
statements.

Siddhartha: What difference do you have in mind?

Dilemma: Take first the ordinary statement, "It is raining out."
In uttering such a statement, I am simply telling you what is the
case. I am saying nothing about how you should act. In contrast,

if I say "Murder is wrong," then I am really saying how you and others should behave. As far as I am concerned it is the same as having said "Thou shalt not kill." Moral pronouncements in general are like that. They are attempts to *command* people, to *direct* their behavior. If this is right, then moral pronouncements are best looked at as a special class of commands or as reports of commands.

Siddhartha: "Commands" and "reports of commands"?

Dilemma: Consider "Thou shalt not kill." Didn't Moses claim that this was a command from God?

Siddhartha: He did.

Dilemma: Well, then, I think it is safe to say that the early Jews looked upon moral norms as commands from God. Accordingly, "Killing is wrong" might be said to be a report of God's command for an ancient Jew, whereas "Thou shalt not kill" expresses the command itself. But looking at the matter from a scientific view, you can't explain what is really going on by looking at the command as issuing from God. The only alternative is to say that the command "Thou shalt not kill" really came from society itself. Society, not God, is the real authority behind the moral command. Society, not God, will punish those who break the moral command. Since different societies issue different moral commands, enforce different moral norms, what is moral is relative to the society in question. So if my theory that a moral pronouncement is simply a special sort of command from society is right, it is futile to look for the one single, right morality, since obviously these special sorts of commands we call morality really do vary from society to society, and that's that.

Siddhartha: I believe your theory is quite mistaken, Dilemma. I don't deny that morality aims at guiding or directing people's behavior, nor that moral pronouncements such as "Thou shalt not kill" and "Murder is wrong" have a force comparable to a command. But none of this shows that they are commands issued by society. The real authority of moral statements to command the truly moral person derives from neither a fear of society nor from a fear of God, but rather out of a respect for doing what is right for the sake of doing what is right. Although it is true that some people do what they think is moral only because they fear that God or society will punish them, this is not the case with someone who is really moral, in my view. For in my view, if someone is really moral they do what is right simply because they believe it is the right thing to do and for no other reason. So for them all they care about is whether or not it is *true* that killing is morally wrong or not.

Dilemma: And I say that truth has nothing to do with it. It is society's rewards and punishments alone that always make people do what their society calls right and avoid doing what their society calls wrong.

Siddhartha: Are you saying that a society can't be mistaken in what norms it enforces, that a society can't have *false* beliefs about what moral norms it should have? Is that what you mean when you say truth has nothing to do with morality?

Dilemma: That's it exactly.

Siddhartha: But how can you explain social reform? Was slavery not morally and legally sanctioned here in America a little over a hundred years ago? And did Americans not come to say that slavery is wrong, that it is a mistake to believe that any human should live in bondage? Great! Slavery strikes again!

Moral progress

Dilemma: What you are talking about is an inconsistency within the set of moral norms themselves. Americans came to see that slavery is wrong or mistaken only in the sense of realizing that it was inconsistent with their Christian and democratic moral norms, which hold that all men are free and equal. So I will admit that a society's moral norms can be mistaken in the sense that they are inconsistent with each other. But that is the only sense in which they can be wrong, and that is something that is compatible with moral relativity. For each society's moral

[handwritten top margin: The only kind of moral error D allows is inconsistency with one's other moral views]

norms have only to be consistent with themselves and not with the moral norms of other societies.

Siddhartha: Nonetheless, we are making progress. For you are already admitting that a society can be mistaken about its moral norms, that it can have *false* beliefs about what norms it should or shouldn't have?

Dilemma: I give you that much but no more, Siddhartha. In the matter of the internal consistency of its norms, a society can be mistaken. But that is all.

Siddhartha: But can't the members of a society rationally examine its norms and find them wanting or defective in other ways?

[handwritten: cf. Shiner!]

Dilemma: What has reason to do with it? Roughly, what a society calls good or right is what the members of that society find reinforcing or rewarding due to their genetic endowment and the natural and social conditions they live in. They can't stand outside their culture and evaluate it from a God-like perspective. Either you do or you don't find it reinforcing or rewarding to follow your society's moral norms. If it is reinforcing or rewarding to obey them, then you obey them. Otherwise you don't. It is not a matter of a rational decision. From a scientific point of view, your society shapes your moral behavior, not you. We are not free in the way required to make such a rational decision as you are suggesting.

Siddhartha: Well then, let me ask you what we are all doing right now.

Dilemma: What do you mean?

Siddhartha: Consider the following description of what the four of us are doing right now: We are engaged in the process of making and listening to various assertions or conclusions for which we are giving reasons or premises. In short, we are formulating and considering various arguments, for an argument is nothing but a conclusion along with its premises. As we

[handwritten bottom margin: D denies poss. of rational evaluation of moral beliefs, using a Shiner-like determinism]

[handwritten annotation at top: S respond by showing that we do rationally evaluate all our beliefs, even moral ones]

proceed with this process, we encounter arguments and counter-arguments, arguments for and against some conclusion, and this enables us to see which arguments are the good ones and which are not as good or not good at all. So in doing this, we are assuming all along an ability on our part to discriminate, at least sometimes, between which arguments are the good ones and which the bad ones. Do you agree with me so far?

Dilemma: I do.

Siddhartha: Then note that as a consequence of this process, some of our beliefs or conclusions will change completely, some will be more or less changed, and still others will remain the same as when we began our discussion. Moreover, as our beliefs change so will our behavior—what we say and do and even what we think to ourselves. Sometimes the changes that occur are trivial, but sometimes they are very important, and occasionally they are even critical. Finally, some of the changes in beliefs that can occur from discussions such as this are changes in beliefs about this or that moral norm. And such a change in belief can result in our willingness to act in accordance with that norm or in our refusal to do so. Can you deny any of this?

Dilemma: I suppose I can't, no.

Siddhartha: Well then, you can't deny that human beings have an ability to rationally evaluate the moral norms of their society. For all I meant in saying this was that they have an ability to entertain arguments pro and con some moral norm of their society, to distinguish the good arguments from the bad, and to accept or reject that norm and act accordingly. You don't wish to deny that humans can do such a thing, do you?

Dilemma: I suppose not.

Siddhartha: That is a good supposition, for to suppose the opposite would put you in an embarrassing position.

Dilemma: How is that?

Siddhartha: Because, you would no sooner suppose the oppo-site, and I would ask you for an argument or reason for your opposite supposition. This would then place you in the embar-rassing position of either not giving an argument because you want to remain consistent with your claim that people aren't rational, or of giving an argument and that would be inconsistent with that claim. For if people are not rational in my sense, then either they can't give or consider arguments at all, or they can't tell the difference between good and bad ones and act accord-ingly.

Dilemma: I see your point. I see I have no choice but to agree with you or make a fool of myself.

Siddhartha: Now that we can agree that humans are rational in the sense I have indicated, we can no longer say it is senseless to ask humans to rationally evaluate the norms of their society because such rationality is beyond them.

Dilemma: I stand corrected on that account. But I still don't see on what grounds beyond internal inconsistency one can say that the norms of a society are wrong or that the people's beliefs about them are mistaken. It still seems to me that beyond internal consistency the only other thing people consider is their feelings, how they feel emotionally about this or that norm. And I don't see how you can argue about feelings. They are a product of conditioning, pure and simple.

Siddhartha: Then you are overlooking people's interests. What I think or feel is in my interest and what really is in my interest may not be the same. I may feel or think it is not in my interest to go to the doctor. Yet I may go to the doctor and discover I have some very serious condition that was caught just in the nick of time. In that case, my feelings about not going to the doctor would have been contrary to my real interest. So when it comes to a person's true interests, reason is frequently a better guide than just feelings. I submit to you, Dilemma, that a second way that the members of a society may be mistaken about their moral norms is that they may believe those norms serve their

Feelings can be mistaken

1. Conceiving what is in our best pragmatic interests
2. Conceiving morality (when it is based on society's interests)

NB. #2 presupposes utilitarian view.

interests when, in fact, they do not. If, for example, any society thought that murder, dishonesty, or thievery were norms that would serve their interests, they would soon discover that they were sadly mistaken.

Dilemma: For the moment you have me cornered, Siddhartha.

Siddhartha: I submit to you therefore that murder, dishonesty, and thievery are universally wrong, Dilemma, while respect for life, honesty, and respect for what belongs to another are universally right. They are morally right and wrong not just because society says they are, but for reasons quite apart from what society says. These things are right and wrong absolutely and not relative to some society.

Dilemma: As I just admitted, you have stumped me for the moment. I think it is time to ask for reinforcements. I am certain there is something wrong with what you have concluded, but at the moment I can't put my finger on it.

Max: Then I will take over for you, Dilemma, for I see how Siddhartha has trapped you.

Dilemma: Good. Please proceed.

S bases his final arg. for moral realism on the
benefit for all societies of honesty, respect for others, etc.
Me: it's a mistake to hinge realism on util., or worse,
enlightened egoism (on a national/worldwide scale)

Part II

Max's Case for Ethical Relativism

Max: I accept all that you have just now said, Siddhartha, when you said a society may be in error about its moral norms, that its beliefs about its moral norms may be mistaken, not only with respect to their internal consistency, but with respect to how well they serve that society's interests as well. But your belief that this provides you with a basis for rejecting moral relativism is quite mistaken.

Siddhartha: Why is that?

Max: Without realizing it both you and Dilemma were using the words 'right', 'wrong', and 'rational' in two different senses, and this is why you were able to corner Dilemma just now.

Siddhartha: What different senses do you have in mind?

Max: First of all take the word 'rational'. As an absolutist, you think that to be rational and to be moral are the same.

Siddhartha: Not quite. You will recall that just a while back I explained that being rational is a matter of being able to follow arguments for and against some conclusion, to discriminate the good from the bad arguments, and to draw conclusions and act accordingly. Since people who are not moral can do such things, I would have to say that they are rational to a certain extent.

However, I do believe that someone who was fully or ideally rational would draw all the right conclusions about morality and would as a consequence act out of moral considerations and so be a moral person. So I would have to say that to be *fully* rational is to be moral, yes.

Max: I accept your qualification. But it does not matter, Siddhartha; for, although you and I have the same concept of rationality, we have very different concepts of morality. Hence, I don't accept your conclusion that to be fully rational is to be moral.

Siddhartha: Would you care to explain yourself?

Max: Yes. To be fully or ideally rational would be to draw all of the right conclusions about morality as you have said. But it does not follow, given my conception of morality, that having drawn all of the right or correct conclusions about morality, one will do the moral thing. This leads us back to the two senses in which you and Dilemma were using the words 'right' and 'wrong'. Although a society may be *wrong* about its moral norms, it can't be said to be *morally wrong* about its moral norms.

Siddhartha: What is the difference?

Max: As you have pointed out, moral norms may be wrong in the sense of failing to serve the people's interests. But this is being *wrong in a nonmoral sense*. It is irrational for a society to have moral norms that are contrary to its interests, but it is not immoral.

Siddhartha: I see. A moral norm that runs counter to a society's interests is wrong in the sense of irrational, but not wrong in a moral sense.

Max: Exactly. In my view, morality consists in the moral norms of a society and absolutely nothing else. To be moral is simply to obey the moral norms of your society and nothing more. Now

Yes! I don't know why S brought up self-interest in the first place. It plays into the hands of the relativist.

Max: Two senses of "[strikethrough] right & 'wrong'"
  1. (Failing to) conforming to society's norms (moral sense)
  2. In one's own self-interest (or society's) (nonmoral sense)
Max's Ethical Relativism   17

if you are rational, then you may sometimes be moral, but not always.

Siddhartha: And under what circumstances will the rational person obey the moral norms of their society and under what circumstances will the rational person not obey them?

Max: It all depends upon how well obeying those norms will serve the rational person's strongest interests and upon how much obeying those same norms will stifle their strongest interests. If in the balance, obeying those moral norms really does serve their interests, they will obey them; while if in the balance obeying those moral norms will really stifle their interests, they will not obey them.

Siddhartha: I see.

Max: Yes. And this leads to my point about the way you and Dilemma were using the words 'right' and 'wrong' just a little while ago. You two were using those words as if they each had only one sense—a moral sense. But for a relativist such as I, there are really two senses in which you were using the words 'right' and 'wrong'—a moral sense and a nonmoral sense. To say that something is right, or wrong, in the moral sense is simply to say that it conforms to society's moral norms, or fails to do so, while to say something is right, or wrong, in the nonmoral sense is simply to say it is rational in the sense I have just explained above. Just a while ago both you and Dilemma were using the words 'right' and 'wrong' in these two different senses without realizing it, and that is why you were able to drive Dilemma into a corner in the way you did.

Siddhartha: When was that?

Max: When you got Dilemma to admit that respect for life, honesty, and respect for what belongs to another are universally right and, similarly, to admit that murder, dishonesty, and thievery are universally wrong. These things are universally right and universally wrong in the nonmoral sense that it is rational for all societies to place restrictions on killing, lying,

Restrictions on killing, dishonesty, etc. are universally valid, is that they are in all society's interests. But which particular restrictions (moral norms) are adopted vary according to the different needs of each society. Moral norms are hence relative, not absolute

and the use of property. But if we consider the actual restrictions—the moral norms themselves—they vary considerably from society to society. Take killing as an example. The Aztecs sacrificed maidens to the Gods; certain South Sea Islanders practiced infanticide; Eskimos used to send their aging parents out to sea on icebergs; and still others practiced cannibalism. In America today all of these practices are illegal and would be considered immoral for Americans to follow. At the other extreme there are the Quakers who look upon our so-called just wars as mass murder. Hence, although it is nonmorally right or rational for all societies to place restrictions upon killing, the particular restrictions or moral norms it is nonmorally right to place upon killing are by no means universal, but vary from culture to culture. It all depends what best serves a society. If cannibalism or infanticide best serves the interest of some society, then they are nonmorally right for that society, and that's that. There is nothing more to be said. For it is senseless to speak of the moral norms themselves as being *morally* right or *morally* wrong as absolutists do.

Siddhartha: What you have just said convinces me that I should pay you back the debt I owe you.

Max: What debt is that?

Siddhartha: The debt I incurred when just now you said I was using the words 'right' and 'wrong' in two different senses. Now that I fully grasp your meaning, I see that I should pay you back in like coin.

Max: How is that?

Siddhartha: Because it is now clear to me that you are using the word 'moral' in two different senses, and that is what has given rise to your theory that I am using the words 'right' and 'wrong' in two different senses.

Max: I will have to be persuaded before I will grant you that.

Siddhartha: Then let me ask you this: As a logician, wouldn't you say that there are two closely related, but distinct senses in which we use the word 'logical'?

Max: What do you have in mind?

Siddhartha: Well, on the one hand, there are the various particular systems of logic such as may be found in logic books. Sometimes we may say that someone's thinking is logical in the sense that their thinking or reasoning satisfies the rules or norms to be found in such a system. Would you agree that that is one sense in which we use the word 'logical'?

Max: I would.

Siddhartha: Yet is it not also true that someone's thinking may be logical in another sense even if it fails to satisfy the rules in any system of logic?

Max: What do you have in mind?

Siddhartha: Consider the following argument:
Once a lady, always a lady.
Alma's no lady.
Therefore Alma never was a lady.
Would you not agree that this is a logically valid argument?

Max: I certainly would, for I recognize it as the sort of argument I have had my students prove valid.

Siddhartha: But suppose you had lived two thousand years ago when Aristotle's was the only logical system around. Would that argument have been found logical by the rules of Aristotle's system?

Max: You know it would not. Only by the rules of modern symbolic logic can we prove the logical validity of such an argument.

Siddhartha: Yet the argument was, in fact, just as logical in Aristotle's time as it is today. Is that not so?

great eg!

Max: Of course.

Siddhartha: So in Aristotle's time the above argument was not logical in the sense of satisfying the rules in some existing system of logic. Yet it was still logical in the deeper sense that it is an example of thinking the way one *ought* to think. Would you agree?

Max: I cannot deny what you say.

Siddhartha: So here we have two distinct senses of the word 'logical'. On the one hand, someone's thoughts or reasoning may be logical in the sense of satisfying the rules of some system of logic. On the other hand, their thoughts or reasoning may be logical in the sense of being the way they ought to be.

Max: I accept your distinction.

Siddhartha: And would you also agree that just as something may be logical in the second sense but not the first, it might also be logical in the first sense but not the second?

Max: I would. For a poorly constructed system of logic might count, as logically valid, arguments that in fact are not logically valid.

Siddhartha: And which of the two senses of logic would you say is more basic and more important?

Max: The second, of course. For in constructing a system of logic in the first place, the primary aim is always to distinguish between thinking or reasoning of the sort people ought to engage in from that they ought not engage in.

Siddhartha: Good. We may then distinguish between three different kinds of thinking: First there is the way people actually argue or think, which is sometimes not logical in either sense. Second, there is argument or thinking that is logical in the sense of satisfying the rules of some logical system. And third, there is thinking that is logical in the sense of thinking as it ought to be—right thinking.

1. Actual reasoning (may be highly illogical)
2. Reasoning according to a system of logic
3. Reasoning according to the optimal system of logic.

Max: I accept those distinctions.

Siddhartha: Now when you as a teacher of logic try to improve your students' actual ways of thinking, you always refer to some system of logic.

Max: Necessarily.

Siddhartha: But you always refer to a system of logic that you believe to be a good one, so that if your students properly follow its rules they will, in fact, be thinking the way they ought to.

Max: Naturally. I would never deliberately use a system of logic unless I thought it was a good one, one that will help my students think or reason the way they ought to.

Siddhartha: I am glad you agree with all I have said, for I am now in a position to explain the two senses in which people use the word 'moral'. Just as we can distinguish between three different kinds of thinking, so too we can distinguish between three different kinds of action. First of all there is the way people actually behave or act. It may not be moral in either sense of the word. Second, there is action that is moral in the sense that it satisfies the rules or norms of some moral system in some society. And third, there is action that is moral in the more fundamental sense of action as it *ought* to be, right action. Just as you teach your students to think according to what you take to be a good system of logic, a logical system that will get them thinking as they ought to, so too conscientious parents teach their children to act according to what they take to be a good system of morals, a moral system that will get them acting as they ought.

Max: I reject your claim that there is any such distinction in the case of the word 'moral', though I accept it in the case of the word 'logical'.

Siddhartha: Then tell me this, Max, what would you say people are arguing about when one of them says that abortion is moral and the other says it is immoral?

Max: They are arguing whether or not having an abortion satisfies or violates the moral norms of their society. *[handwritten: the majority think]*

[handwritten: majority may be wrong. Moral debate about issue, not what]

Siddhartha: But that surely can't be right. For in that case, we should resolve such arguments by simply taking a poll or conducting some other sort of sociological investigation. I have no doubt that neither side of the debate over abortion, for example, would be satisfied with the sociologist's findings, no matter what they were. When one side says abortion is immoral and the other that it is moral, they are not simply talking about what society thinks about the matter—that society takes it to be immoral or moral. They are talking about whether or not it really is immoral or moral, a matter about which they would say society might be mistaken.

Max: But I would draw a distinction between what society takes to be moral and what satisfies the moral norms of society. You are right that society can be mistaken in what it takes to be moral in a given instance. Just as I may be mistaken in thinking some particular argument or reasoning satisfies my system of logic, so too society may be mistaken in thinking some particular kind of action, such as abortion, satisfies its system of morals. A lot of people in this country, for example, once thought that slavery was perfectly consistent with their Judeo-Christian/democratic principles; but now just about everyone agrees they were mistaken. Hence, I say that when people argue about the morality of things such as slavery or abortion, they are arguing about the consistency of such actions with society's moral system.

Siddhartha: I don't deny they are arguing that, Max. I simply deny that that is *all* they are arguing about. For consider a case where you are mistaken in thinking that some argument satisfies your system of logic. Why does that bother you? Is it not because you take this as demonstrating that the argument or reasoning in question is not as it ought to be? Do you not assume that its failing to be logical in the sense of failing to satisfy your logical system shows it also fails to be logical in the deeper sense of failing to be thinking or reasoning as it ought to be?

[handwritten: Internal consistency with logical/moral principles is only of interest because system is believed to be correct/defensible]

Max: That is true.

Siddhartha: Well my suggestion is that it is the same with regard to moral arguments. The reason people in this country were concerned with whether or not slavery was compatible with Judeo-Christian ethics is because they believed that system of ethics to be the right one. Someone who did not accept those principles as the right ones in the first place would scarcely care whether or not some action or practice was consistent with them. They would have referred to a different system of morals—the one they subscribe to. When people say something is moral, they generally don't mean simply that it satisfies the norms of their society's moral system, but that it satisfies the norms of the moral system they believe in—the right moral system, or the moral system their society ought to subscribe to. This is obvious, in fact, in the case of most Christians and Jews.

Max: How is that?

Siddhartha: Most pious Christians or Jews will tell you that the norms or principles they subscribe to are right, not simply because they say they are or because some society says they are right, but rather because those principles or norms are firmly grounded in a higher reality, the source of all being. It is only too obvious in such cases that when they say something is moral or immoral, they mean much more than that it is consistent with the norms of their society's moral system.

Max: Then I must say that they are mistaken, for there is no higher reality of the sort they assume.

Siddhartha: But that is not the point. Say they are mistaken in what they *believe* if you wish. The issue concerns what they *mean.* And the point is that when they say something is moral they *mean* much more than that it satisfies the norms of their society. Nor are Christians and Jews using the word 'moral' in an unusual way. To the contrary, they are using it in the standard way ordinary people use that word. For in fact when ordinary people say that something is moral, they ordinarily mean *some-*

thing more than that it satisfies the norms of their society's moral system.

Max: For the sake of argument, Siddhartha, I shall grant you your semantical point and agree that there are two distinct senses of the word 'moral'. What do you think follows if I grant you that point?

Siddhartha: Well, let us first of all agree on some way of keeping these two senses of morality distinct so that we don't confuse them as we talk about them. Since being moral *simply* in the sense of satisfying some system of morals is not what people argue about or mean when they try to decide how they should live, let us refer to being moral in this sense as being moral in a *secondary sense*. In contrast, when it is being moral in the really important sense, the action-guiding sense that people argue about and care about, that we are speaking of, let us call this being moral in the *primary sense*.

Max: I accept your proposal. Now what do you say follows from this distinction between the word 'moral' in the secondary and in the primary senses?

Siddhartha: For one thing, the argument you have been presenting on behalf of relativism will not do at all.

Max: What argument is that?

Siddhartha: I would characterize your central argument for relativism roughly as follows: "What satisfies a society's moral system is relative to a given society. What satisfies a society's moral system is what is moral for that society. Therefore, what is moral for a given society is relative to that society." Can you deny that this is how you have been arguing?

Max: No, I cannot.

Siddhartha: Then here I think is where I can make good my claim that you have used the word 'moral' in two distinct senses. When you used the word 'moral' in your second premise, you were using it in the way we have agreed to call the secondary sense, the unimportant sense. But when you used the word 'moral' in your conclusion, you were using it in our primary sense, the sense in which people argue when one says something is moral and the other denies this. For unless you have been meaning to speak of the word 'moral' in this primary sense in your conclusion, your thesis of moral relativism is entirely trivial and uninteresting and not worth two minutes' discussion. But this means that the argument you have been assuming all along is guilty of the fallacy of equivocation, since it rests upon a shift in the meaning of the word 'moral'.

Max: I see. And is that all or is there more?

Siddhartha: Only one thing more. When Dilemma and I were using the words 'right' and 'wrong' a little while ago, we were not, as you thought, using them in a moral and nonmoral sense. We were, rather, using them in a single sense, the primary moral sense.

Max: Then for the sake of argument, I will accept your distinction between the two senses of the word 'moral' and all that you say follows from it. For I shall soon show you it does not matter. It will only complicate my defense of relativism and not undermine it in any way.

Siddhartha: Then I am your willing student.

Max: Earlier you compelled Dilemma to admit that a society may be mistaken about the moral norms it has, not simply with respect to their internal consistency with one another, but with respect to how well they serve the interests of society. You will perhaps recall that I agreed with you on this point.

Siddhartha: I do.

Max: At the time, however, I insisted that to be right or wrong about moral norms in this way is to be nonmorally right or wrong. I took the position that the interests of society are a nonmoral good and that what serves those interests is nonmorally right.

Siddhartha: I recall your taking that position.

Max: Well now that, for the sake of argument, I am willing to say that there are two senses of the word 'moral', I will revise my theory. I shall agree to call the interests of society a moral good, and I shall say that whatever serves the interests of society is morally right in what you call the primary sense of the word 'moral'. I think you can see how this will enable me to account for what two people are arguing about when one says something is moral and the other says it is immoral.

Siddhartha: I have an idea of what you might say, but I would like you to tell me all the same, so that I can be sure.

Max: When two people are arguing over whether or not something is moral, they are concerned with the interests of society. For example, when one party argues that abortion is morally right, they are arguing that it is in the interests of society, while their opponent is arguing just the opposite. So to argue about what is moral in your primary sense is simply to argue about what is truly in the interests of society.

Siddhartha: I see.

Max: This enables me to explain your three kinds of actions. A person is doing something immoral in both senses if the action is both contrary to the norms of society and contrary to the interests of society as well. An action may be moral in the secondary sense if it simply satisfies the system of moral norms of society, whether or not it is truly in the interests of that society. Finally, an action may be said to be moral in the primary sense if it is in the true interests of some society, whether or not it conforms to the system of moral norms of the society in question.

Siddhartha: And exactly how do you propose to defend relativism on this view?

Max: Easily. It follows from the nature of human interests.

Siddhartha: What do you mean?

M allows objectivity, in that ~~a~~ society can be mistaken about what is in its best interests. This allows for 'primary' moral errors. But it's far removed from universal morality.

M tries to reduce all moral concern (from egoism to altruism) to various interests, which are themselves genetically/environmentally determined

So primary morality depends on needs of each society

Max's Ethical Relativism   27

Max: Just consider the enormous range of human interests. At one extreme, for example, there are those whose only interests are in themselves. Let us call these people selfish. At another extreme, there are those who have interest in an immense number of other people and other things besides themselves and whose interests in things and people other than themselves are even stronger than their interest in themselves. Let us call these people selfless. Most people are at various points between these two extremes—having all manner of various interests. Moreover, people's interests, both selfish and nonselfish, vary immensely. One person may have a selfish interest in glory, another a selfish interest in wealth. Or again, one person may have a nonselfish interest in ecology, another an unselfish interest in feeding the millions of starving people around the globe. It is hard to imagine anything more plastic and variable than human interests.

Siddhartha: And what conclusions do you draw from all of this?

Max: It is rather clear to me that people's interests, apart from being partially determined by their genetic endowment, are mostly shaped by the human and nonhuman environment into which they are born. Their human environment or their culture is particularly decisive in this respect, so that people's true interests will vary enormously from culture to culture. But this means that what is in the true interests of society will vary enormously from society to society and so therefore will what is moral in the primary sense as well. Thus, if it was truly in the interests of the Eskimos to send their aging parents out to sea, for the South Sea Islanders to practice infanticide, and for the cannibals to eat people, then it was also moral for them to do these things, even though it would not be in the true interests, that is moral, for Americans to do these same things. So as you can see, Siddhartha, moral relativism once more raises its glorious head.

Siddhartha: I do not deny that relativism is a many-headed creature, and now I can see why you think your admitting to two senses of the word 'moral' still permits you to maintain your moral relativism.

Max: Not only that. I can still maintain my claim that it is possible to be completely rational and still not be moral.

Siddhartha: How is that?

Max: Consider the case of the completely selfish person, one whose only interest is in her own self with no interest in anybody or anything else, including society. If she had her way, she would have everyone serving her interests and nothing else. Now given this selfish nature and given that what is moral is what serves the interests of society, something she is indifferent to, there is no reason or rational grounds for her to care about doing what is moral, except when doing so serves some one of her various selfish interests. Thus, she might do what is moral in order to avoid being punished by society or because the moral act is in her selfish interest in some other way. But never, if she is rational, will she do the moral thing simply because that is what serves the interests of society.

Siddhartha: I see. And what about others?

Max: In the case of others, it will depend upon if and to what extent they take an interest in the interests of society as a whole. If the interests of society as a whole conflict with some other interest they have, whether in themselves or in something or someone else, then it will depend which in that particular case represents their stronger interest. If it is the interest of society that constitutes their stronger interest, then it will be rational for them to go with that and do what is moral. But if it is the other interest that is their stronger interest, then it will be more rational for them to serve that other interest, even though this would be the immoral thing to do.

Siddhartha: I think I now understand your view. What is moral, in the primary sense, is that which serves the interests of society, but what is rational is that which serves the strongest or most important interests of the individual. So in those cases

A selfish individual may be rational in doing what is immoral, in the sense of not being in society's interest *(handwritten note at top of page: "Max: rational = egoistic (which may violate sometimes being apparently altruistic)")*

where the individual's strongest or most important interest happens to be in doing that which promotes the interests of society as a whole, it is rational for him to be moral. But in those cases where the individual's strongest interest is something else, something that conflicts with the interests of society, then in that case it is rational for him to do the immoral thing. Is that your view?

Max: It is. So in my view, a highly moral person is simply someone whose strongest interest is in society, while a highly immoral person is simply one whose strongest interest is rarely or never what is in the interest of society. Both kinds of people, as well as all of those in between, however, may be said to be fully rational persons if they are faithful to their real interests and pursue them in reasonable ways.

Siddhartha: Tell me then, Max, if morality can be so easily turned aside whenever it conflicts with some interest that happens to be stronger, what is it that keeps society as stable as it is so that it does not turn into a complete jungle with people constantly at one another's throats?

Max: First of all, keep in mind the rather grim fact that society sometimes is like a jungle, as constant wars and criminal activity frequently remind us. Second, the order that exists in society is not based upon morality alone by any means. Most people realize that a disorderly jungle would be contrary to their own selfish interests as well as to their interests in other things and people, such as family and friends. So they gladly support the government, army, and police—not simply to secure the interests of society as a whole, but to secure their other interests as well. Even the perfectly selfish person benefits from having law and order. And that is not all either. *(handwritten note: "enlightened egoism")*

Siddhartha: What else is there?

Max: In addition to governments that officially impose penalties upon law-breakers, there are also the informal sanctions that all of us impose upon one another when we or someone else cf. Shiver!

violates the moral norms of society. Morally good behavior or behavior that is deemed to be in the interests of society, moreover, is praised and rewarded in other ways in order to keep everyone in line. Theoretically, a nation of selfish devils could be extremely orderly, not because any individual cared about society as a whole, but simply because each devil realized it was in his own selfish interest to maintain an orderly society by means of force. Hence, each selfish devil would submit to the rules of his society, not because he wanted to do so himself, but rather only because he wanted everyone else to do so.

Siddhartha: I think you are quite right about that, Max. So long as they could arrange things so that wrongdoing was efficiently punished and right action properly and duly rewarded, they could count on everyone's selfish interests to lead them to act in ways that served the interests of society as a whole.

Max: Then you agree that my views about morality do not imply that society must necessarily be a disorderly jungle.

Siddhartha: I certainly do. However, I think that from what you said earlier you will agree that although the actions of such selfish devils would outwardly conform to the requirements of morality, they would not be genuinely moral actions. Am I right about this?

Max: You are indeed. For as I said earlier, to be moral is to not simply act in the interests of society, but to act out of an interest in the interests of society, and not out of some other kind of interest, selfish or otherwise. Therefore, since these selfish devils would only do what is moral because they were afraid of getting caught or because they were looking for some selfish reward, they could not be said to be moral even if they always did what was moral.

Siddhartha: Now that I understand how, from your view, it is possible to have law and order, I would like to raise one final question about your view: How can you explain moral obligation?

M's system of enlightened egoism misses the point of morality

Max: I don't think I quite understand your question.

Siddhartha: Then let me explain: I believe it is a part of the notion of moral obligation that someone is bound to do the moral thing regardless of whatever particular interests they happen to have or what their circumstances happen to be. What is moral is supposed to override every other consideration, no matter what that consideration might be. If something really is the moral thing to do, it is to be done, period. Nothing else matters. My question then is this: How, in your view, is it possible for people to have such moral obligations?

Max: Let us suppose that moral obligation is as you have just now explained it. In my view, this is to be explained in terms of accountability. Consider again the nation of selfish devils. If they are rational, they are not going to say to one another: "Everyone must obey our moral and legal norms, but only when they are interested in doing so." If they said that, no one would ever act in accord with the moral, legal norms because each is a selfish devil. And each one of them would know this. Accordingly, to make the whole thing work they would have to say the following to one another: "Everyone must unconditionally obey our moral and legal norms." And this is what they would say. What would hold true for a nation of selfish devils would equally hold true for actual, human societies that are made up of some completely selfish people and some highly selfless people, but mostly of people at various points between these two extremes. For us too, the moral order can only be upheld by our insisting that morality have the highest priority—that moral considerations always override all other considerations. Hence, the unconditionality of moral obligation simply arises from the fact that a society must say to itself that moral considerations must override all others, or there will be no moral order at all. That is society's point of view. Nonetheless, from the individual's point of view it is only rational to do what is moral if that is what serves one's strongest interests.

Siddhartha: If I understand you correctly, you are saying that there are two distinct points of view; one when we are acting as

"noble lie" needed to retain order

Society must enforce / insist on obedience to morality; but it is frequently not intrinsic to the advantage of individuals (& is hence irrational) to Part II *obey moral rules.*

32

society's legislators, and one when we are acting as *individual agents.* As rational legislators, our interest is in promoting a certain kind of world or society. Even selfish devils can assume this viewpoint. And when they do they can see the need to give the highest priority to what is moral. On the other hand, when the individual is acting on her own behalf as a rational agent, she sees that it is, in fact, rational for her to make an exception of herself and go against society's moral rules, the very rules she herself would advocate from her view as a legislator.

Max: That is it exactly. To return to my example of the nation of selfish devils, one could imagine a selfish devil among them who was extremely clever and who constantly went against the very moral and legal norms he helped promote whenever it suited him and whenever he could get away with it. From the legislative point of view, it would be irrational to allow others to make exceptions of themselves, since he wants them to always do right by him and in general to promote an orderly and peaceful world. But from his individual point of view, as an agent, it would be irrational for him to secretly not make an exception of himself whenever it was in his interest to do so, and he wouldn't get caught in doing so. Given his selfish interests, he would be acting in an entirely consistent way in embracing both perspectives, because in both cases, as a legislator and as an agent, he would always be serving his own selfish interests, and I can find nothing irrational nor inconsistent in that. When people are talking about moral obligation, they are talking about something that is rationally required from the legislator's point of view, not from the agent's point of view.

Siddhartha: But this won't do, for moral obligation is something we feel as rational agents and not merely something that we deem rational or necessary from the legislative point of view. For to feel moral obligation as a rational agent is precisely to feel that we must not make an exception in our own case, that what we rationally require of others, we must equally require of ourselves. If what you say is right, then it can *never* be rational to have such a feeling. In your view, unless I already happen to

"Moral pull" is felt independently of whether it's in our self-interest. M's account fails to do justice to this fundamental fact of our experience. M bites the bullet & admits that moral pull is a mystery, based on an illusion.

have an interest in doing what the moral law requires of me, it can't rationally compel me. So the obligation I feel must be a complete illusion. For if I already have an overriding interest in doing what morality requires of me, I will not feel compelled; while if morality requires me to do what is contrary to my strongest interest, then the feeling of compulsion must be irrational. Hence, the feeling of being compelled by the moral law, or the feeling of being bound by it, must either be absent or be irrational.

Max: In the interests of rendering my account of morality in keeping with science, I am willing to accept such consequences. For a moral obligation that can compel the agent apart from her particular interests is a mystery to me and something I hold can't be squared with a scientific or naturalistic account of morality.

Siddhartha: Then it seems to me that in your view, those who act out of purely moral motives, doing what is morally right simply for its own sake, are really no better than the worst scoundrels. For in your view, it must be a matter of mere accident that those who are moral have the interests they have and, similarly, it is purely accidental that the selfish scoundrels have the interests they have. Or even if being moral versus being selfish is a matter of choice, in your view, it must be a choice wholly without reasons, for one can't say, except from within the moral point of view itself, that it is really better to be one way or the other.

Max: If that follows from my view, then I accept that also.

Siddhartha: Then as far as I am concerned, your view, rather than explaining true morality, eliminates it.

M's view entails that the moral life is groundless & that the decision to lead it rather than to pursue self-interest is arbitrary. So M really advocates amoralism

Part III

Homer's Case for Ethical Relativism

Homer: I hope you will excuse me for breaking in on the two of you like this, but I must say, Max, that I think you are mistaken to agree with Siddhartha that you cannot account for the rationality of moral obligation from the agent's point of view.

Max: Your comments are always welcome, Homer. Please tell us where you think I have let Siddhartha lead me astray and how, without forsaking relativism and science, I can make sense of moral obligation, even from the agent's point of view.

Homer: Is that agreeable to you, Siddhartha?

Siddhartha: By all means. We can use all of the help we can get.

Homer: Well, first I need to understand your views a bit more clearly, Max.

Max: What do you have in mind?

Homer: What you would say about the agent's feeling of moral obligation itself. You have said that this feeling of moral obligation is an illusion.

Max: Yes.

Homer: I take it that you don't wish to deny that the feeling itself is real.

Max: Definitely not. I can hardly deny that people, in fact, experience such feelings. For if they claim to experience such feelings, I am hardly in a position to deny that this is so. In fact, I myself have experienced such feelings, and I know firsthand that the experience of such feelings is real enough.

Homer: Then just what do you mean when you say such feelings are illusions?

Max: I mean that although the agent's experience of having a feeling of moral obligation, apart from her interests, is real enough, the belief to which those feelings give rise, namely the belief that she has a moral obligation, is false. Or to put it another way, the felt moral obligation only *seems* rational, but in fact it is not. It is the cousin to feeling guilty about something it is irrational to feel guilty about. One feels, rationally, that one has done something about which to feel guilty, but careful, rational examination provides no explanation for what is felt.

Homer: So, it is something like seeing a stick in the water that appears to be bent, but is really straight. Someone who did not know better would say that the stick is really bent. Although the experience of seeing the stick look bent is real and undeniable, the belief to which that experience has given rise—namely the belief that the stick is, in fact, bent—is false. Hence, we call it an illusion, since things are other than they appear to be, as in cases where people feel they have a moral obligation, although no interest of theirs is served. Here, too, you are saying that things are not what they appear to be, that, rationally speaking, they have no moral obligation in such cases.

Max: That is my claim exactly.

Homer: Then let us consider the status of your claim for a moment. Suppose you were an anthropologist living with a tribe of people whom you were studying, and that one day you were walking in the forest with a native informant who was teaching you all about his people. The two of you come to a brook and spot a native arrow in the water. Your native informer tells you that the arrow is bent. You say otherwise. You tell him that this is an illusion, that the arrow only appears to be bent, but is really straight. But your friend still disagrees with you. How would you convince him that the stick really is straight?

Max: I would simply pull the arrow out of the water and show him it was really straight.

Homer: Suppose he laughs and explains to you that things bend when they are placed in water, but straighten out again when removed from the water. How in that case would you show him he is wrong?

Max: That would complicate my task enormously, for now I'd have to explain some basic principles of optics and rigid bodies and hope he'd understand and accept these principles.

Homer: So in a word you'd have no recourse but to try and defeat his theory about things bending in water by means of your theories, which you think are better, about optics and rigid bodies?

Max: That's right.

Homer: But suppose instead of having this very debate with a member of some tribe, you encountered the very same debate with an extraterrestrial whose physics was advanced enough to permit him to have travelled from our nearest star, which is four light years away from earth. If someone coming from a culture whose physics is that much more advanced than ours told you that objects bend in water, would you be as confident that your theories were the right ones?

Max: Certainly not. In this case, I'd be more inclined to assume he was right in what he said, although I would still want to see in detail what sort of physics he had.

Homer: Good. I think we can agree, then, that the claim that something is an illusion may be more complex than it might at

A view - factual or moral - cannot be dismissed as an illusion unless a theory can explain why it is illusory.

first appear, and that in any case it is a claim that can often be resolved only by deciding who has the better theory.

Max: Your point is well taken, Homer.

Homer: I am glad we agree on that point. For I think I can offer you a theory that is entirely in keeping with your notions of moral relativity, a theory that will enable you to see that the feeling of moral obligation is no illusion, even in those cases where doing the moral thing serves no particular interest of the agent's.

Max: And just how do you propose to accomplish all of this?

Homer: By picking up on a point that Siddhartha compelled Dilemma to admit, and that you also agreed to.

Max: And what is that?

Homer: The fact that we humans are rational animals, capable of guiding our lives and actions on the basis of reasoned beliefs about what is good and bad, right and wrong.

Max: And what follows from that?

Homer: By virtue of our capacity to reason in this way, we enjoy a certain kind of freedom and a certain kind of responsibility. We are capable of looking at our lives as a totality and of asking ourselves what it is to live a meaningful or worthwhile life and whether or not we are doing this. And we can, accordingly, pursue the worthwhile life, guided by our vision of the worthwhile life in the choices we make each day through the course of our lives. So far as I can see, no other animal on earth is capable of doing this. I cannot, for example, imagine my dog, wonderful as she is, asking herself Hamlet's question "To be or not to be?" So in having this capacity to reason, we enjoy a certain freedom that other animals do not appear to enjoy. But this very freedom also entails the burden of responsibility. For animals, who are guided by instinct and by conditioning alone, nature is the cause of what they become, while we who are capable of being guided by our own reason can blame only ourselves for what we make of ourselves and for what we become. We are without excuses.

Max: I am less certain than you about the extent of our responsibility in what we become. But I suspect that the exact amount of our responsibility is secondary and not relevant to what you are going to say.

Homer: You are right about that. The centrally important fact is that we can, to some extent at least, determine the worth or meaning our lives will have by means of the reasoned choices we make. Now, it is important to see that when we consider the question of the worth of our lives, we can do so from two distinct perspectives.

Max: What do you have in mind?

Homer: On the one hand, we can evaluate the worth of our lives from a subjective perspective, which is to say, in terms of the quality of our consciously lived experiences during the course of our lives. On the other hand, we can evaluate the worth of our lives from an objective perspective, which is to say, in terms of the worth our life has not merely as we see it or experience it, but as others see it or experience it. Looking at our lives from both of these perspectives is inescapable and inevitable for rational beings such as ourselves.

Max: How is that?

Homer: Let's consider the subjective perspective first. Suppose you had the following choices: Either you could spend two weeks cracking rocks ten hours a day on a chain gang and earn two hundred dollars, or you could spend those same two weeks going on the vacation of your choosing with any friends of your choosing, no matter what the cost. Which option would you choose if you had to choose one or the other?

Max: I would naturally choose the vacation.

Homer: Naturally. Suppose, however, you were told that in both cases you would be completely unconscious for the entire two weeks. Let us suppose that in both cases you would be injected with a serum that allowed you to function biologically and behaviorally just as you normally do, but that you would be completely unconscious. Other people would not realize this, since you would do and say everything you normally would do and say. Would this influence your choice?

Max: It certainly would. But let me just clarify a few points. First of all, would my friends be able to enjoy the vacation even though I could not?

Homer: Let us assume they would be injected with the same serum and so like you would be entirely unconscious too.

Max: Second, would I run any risks in choosing the chain gang, for example of having a heart attack, getting murdered, or the like?

Homer: None at all. The serum would protect your health, and it would be seen that no other harm could come to you.

Max: Under the conditions you describe, I would have to reverse my original choice. For I see that in both cases, it would be like going to sleep for two weeks. But in the case of the chain gang I'd get two hundred dollars. In the case of the vacation I'd get nothing.

Homer: I think anyone would agree that you were wise to reverse your original choice. Your original choice was reasonable only in light of the differences the consciously lived experiences of the two options entailed. When we imagined you to have no such consciously lived experiences, this clearly weighted matters in favor of the chain gang. So I think it should be evident that our consciously lived experiences play a very important role in the choices we make in our daily lives.

Max: I can't deny that.

Homer: Then just imagine how this applies to your life as a whole. Suppose, for example, an angel came to you and offered you exactly the life of your choosing for however long you wished it. Such an offer would certainly be irresistible. Would it not?

Max: Yes, it would.

Homer: But suppose the angel then added that, although you'd be perfectly functional biologically and behaviorally, throughout it all you'd be utterly unconscious. That would be the spoiler, wouldn't it?

Max: It certainly would, for so far as I am concerned, under that condition I might as well be dead.

Homer: Or again, it would be equally a spoiler if the angel made that exact same offer to you, but said that instead of not being conscious at all, you'd experience the deepest torment you can imagine—in spite of your getting everything you wanted.

Max: That would be a fate even worse than death.

Homer: Can we safely agree then that the subjective point of view or our concern over the quality of our consciously lived experiences throughout our lives is both inevitable and inescapable so long as we are alive, conscious, and rational?

Max: We certainly can. But we still have what you described as the objective viewpoint to consider. What about that?

Homer: As I said earlier, from the objective perspective we are looking at the worth of our lives not simply from the point of view of us who consciously live those lives, but from a common or public perspective from which many others besides ourselves may view the worth of our lives. Evaluating our lives from such an objective perspective is just as inevitable and inescapable as evaluating our lives from the subjective perspective.

Max: How is that?

Homer: Can you think of anyone who does not care what others think of them, especially what others whom they think highly of think of them?

we also concerned about how other people view us

Max: I must say that I find it hard to believe that anyone is completely indifferent to what others think of them.

Homer: And does not this interest we take in what others think of us reflect something yet deeper?

Max: What do you have in mind?

Homer: Consider the following: Suppose you were an aspiring young musician, and you received very high praise from two different people. Let us say that the first person was simply a man you met on the street who knew little about music. The second person, on the other hand, was a great musician and was, in fact, the musician you admired above all others. Whose praise would you value most, that of the stranger who does not know music or that of the great musician?

Max: Although I would value the praise of both men, I would naturally value the praise of the great musician more.

Homer: And why is that?

Max: Because I would assume he is a better judge, indeed, the very best judge, of whose music is praiseworthy.

Homer: In other words his praise is a clearer indication that you are a praiseworthy musician. Is that it?

Max: That's it exactly.

Homer: Well then, don't you see that we really seek praise because we take it to be an indication that we are praiseworthy and not for itself alone?

Max: I see what you mean. It is being praiseworthy and not praise by itself that we really seek.

Homer: That's right. And similarly, in seeking to be honored, liked, admired, and the like we are really seeking to be honorable, likeable, or admirable. In general, the reason we want people to think highly of us is because we really want to be worthy of high regard, and the reason we don't want people to think little or nothing of us is because we really don't want to be worthy of low regard or to be worthless. As rational animals, humans need to feel that their existence amounts to something, that they are worthy. And that points to something beyond the quality of our consciously lived experience.

Max: And what is that?

Homer: It points to the way in which our lives touch the lives of others. To really be worthy of high regard is something beyond the quality of our consciously lived experience of our life or what is generally called happiness. It is to conduct our lives in a way that makes us worthy of happiness.

Max: What is the difference?

Homer: There is no contradiction in saying that someone is both a complete scoundrel and yet completely happy. But it would be a contradiction to say that someone is a complete scoundrel and is yet completely worthy of happiness. To have the circumstances and means to be happy are one thing; to be worthy of being happy, quite another. A person's happiness often depends in great measure upon what is gotten from society, but worthiness of happiness depends entirely upon what that person gives to society. What makes a musician's music praiseworthy is precisely in what it gives to others or to society at large. The greater the gift the musician bestows on society, the greater the musician. When people think about their happiness, they frequently think in terms of getting, but when society thinks about the worth of someone's life, they think about what that person gave to others. From the objective point of view, our lives are measured in terms of what we give, not in terms of what we get.

Max: I think I see what you mean.

Homer: Moreover, those who are honorable or moral give the highest gift of all to a society, for morality is the very foundation upon which the whole of society rests.

Objective point of view, from which we want to be
morally esteemed (ie. praised because we deserve it),
also very immoral

44   Part III

Max: How is that?

Homer: Well, consider your nation of selfish devils, Max. As you pointed out, they could, in theory at least, use force to get everyone to completely conform to the demands of morality. But they would not thereby be moral, as you yourself have noted. I would only add that they would not therefore constitute a genuine society. For if a people is united only by individual selfish purposes and not by any common purpose, in my judgment, they do not constitute a true society. By contrast, moral conduct motivated in the interests of society as a whole provides an overriding purpose that harmonizes all other purposes and thereby provides the indispensable condition for a genuine society. Hence, by being moral and so setting an example and inspiring others to be moral, the moral individual bestows the highest gift of all upon society, the very gift without which society itself would not be possible. To be worthy of happiness is, above all else, to be moral or, what amounts to the same thing, to be honorable. Above all else, when we consider our lives from the objective point of view, we are considering them from the moral point of view, and we are asking if we are morally worthy of being happy.

Max: Now that I understand what you mean by the objective point of view, I think I am willing to agree that what you say is true of most people, since most people, as far as I can see, take morality seriously. But you have said that you think this point of view, no less than the subjective point of view, is inevitable and inescapable. I have my doubts about that. For example, what about someone who is so severely retarded that he doesn't even have a language?

Homer: There are sad cases where, for some reason, an individual has been denied the full realization of his humanity. For I deem it is quite essential to being human to be capable of rational thinking, and I see no way that this is possible without language. How, without language, can a person think about the world, existence, death, right and wrong, or the nature and meaning of one's own life and humanity? Such people cannot at all entertain either the subjective or the objective point of view. When I say that the subjective and objective points of view are inevitable and inescapable, I mean that they are inevitable and inescapable to the extent that the individual leads a rational life.

Max: But what about superintelligent scoundrels? Are they not supremely rational?

Homer: They are rational, but not supremely rational. They only apply their great intelligence to special tasks and not to every aspect of their lives. Consequently, they are only rational in very limited ways and in very limited areas. To be supremely rational is to be rational about every important facet of one's life, both from a subjective and objective point of view.

Max: And where, in particular, do they fail to be rational in your estimation of matters?

Homer: They are not rational when it comes to the objective point of view, for they are confused about such matters.

Max: Why do you say that?

Homer: Consider the things they place above morality.

Max: Such as?

Homer: Such as wealth, power, and fame.

Max: Suppose the scoundrels tell you these things matter more than being moral?

Homer: I have no doubt they would say just that, and that's why I say they are confused.

Max: Upon what grounds? Your own values?

Homer: Not at all. In terms of their own values or in terms of the common values that are logically implicit in the objective point of view.

Max: I don't think I follow you.

Homer: Well, consider wealth as an example. First of all, tell me why you think we humans value wealth when we consider it from the subjective point of view?

Max: That is not hard to see. Wealth can provide us with things that give us pleasure, on the one hand, and also with things that can help us avert pain and suffering, on the other. That's why we favor it from the subjective point of view.

Homer: Good. And why do you think wealth also appears to be attractive from the objective point of view?

Max: I am not sure.

Homer: Well, is it not true that wealthy people are always surrounded by flatterers and people who think they are wonderful simply because they are wealthy? Do they not also receive all sorts of praise and honors from charitable organizations who are interested in their wealth?

Max: That is quite true.

Homer: Hence, having great wealth comes to be an indication of being a praiseworthy and honorable person in the minds of those who do not examine things with great care.

Max: I can't deny that.

Homer: Yet those who look into matters a bit more deeply and carefully realize that having wealth is not always a trustworthy indicator of a truly noble character. For when it is inherited, the wealthy person too often escapes the very stresses and hardships that make for the highest character. On the other hand, those who attain wealth on their own, though generally strong and clever, frequently compromise what is moral in order to accumulate great wealth. Very frequently they become obsessive and compulsive in their pursuit of wealth, doing great harm to themselves and to others. Those who do not reflect carefully on these matters are likely to be dazzled by wealth as a child might be dazzled by tinsel. They are seduced into believing that, objectively speaking, wealth is a sure sign of a superior character, when often the very opposite is the case.

Max: Is it here then that the scoundrel's confusion comes into the picture, according to you?

Homer: That's exactly right. From a subjective point of view, the scoundrel rightly sees that wealth can be very useful. But he also wrongly thinks that to be wealthy puts him among the highest sort of humans—persons of great superiority. It is here that scoundrels succumb to the illusion that simply having great wealth is equivalent to having the most praiseworthy character. Driven by this belief, they are willing to sacrifice everything and everyone in order to be wealthy because being wealthy is falsely equated with being praiseworthy.

Max: But who is Homer to say they are wrong?

Homer: My claim does not stand on my authority, for I have no authority. I shall put my case to you plain and simple and let you decide for yourself: As I have said, the most praiseworthy musician is the one who gives the most to society. And that is true of anyone—doctor, farmer, or businessman. Whoever gives the most to society is the most praiseworthy, the one society would most rightly honor. But above all are those who make society possible, those who are moral. They deserve the highest praise of all. It follows that to sacrifice morality for wealth in hopes of thereby becoming worthy of the highest praise is to display the gravest sort of confusion and to be guided by a deadly illusion. For to do that is to be the very opposite of honorable and praiseworthy.

Max: And you would say similar things about fame and power, I suppose?

Homer: That's right. Like wealth, fame and power can also help you secure certain pleasures and protect you against certain kinds of pain and suffering. So they can be useful from a subjective point of view.

Max: But from an objective point of view they too are at best weak indicators of the highest sort of character. And in any case, anyone who sacrifices morality for these things in hopes of being the most worthy of praise is pursuing a kind of illusion. For these persons are, in reality, the least worthy of praise. Is that it?

Homer: Well said. And since the scoundrels are the very people who make such sacrifices, I say they are one and all confused.

Max: But aren't you forgetting another sort of scoundrel?

Homer: What sort is that?

Max: Those who are scoundrels out of desperation, people who are poor and, resenting their condition, take to a life of crime.

Homer: I would not call these people scoundrels, Max. They are as confused in their own way as the scoundrel, if not more so. But they are not striving to be better than everyone else, but only to be as good. Like the scoundrel, they in their own way associate the good life with money, power, and wealth. But in their case it is more understandable.

Max: Why do you say that?

Homer: Have you ever been seriously deprived of anything? Food or water?

Max: Yes.

Homer: And haven't you noted how it was hard to think about anything else at such times?

Max: I have. There is a tendency to think, "If only I had some water, or whatever is seriously lacking, that would be the most wonderful thing in the world."

Homer: That's it exactly. Deprivation makes people overvalue that of which they are deprived. The poor are deprived of money, power, and praise or honors. They are looked down upon and badly treated. It is little wonder that they are inclined to overestimate these very things that they desperately lack. So although they are wrong to turn to immoral ways to get what they need, I would not apply the term 'scoundrels' to them.

Max: In any case, you have answered my question, for I see that you would say that they, no less than the scoundrels, are confused about what is important.

Homer: That is my view of the matter. For remember, there are many who, in spite of their poverty, know that being moral matters above all else and who live out their lives with a quiet dignity more noble than that of the most lofty kings. For they are moral when it is hardest to be that way. For this reason, their nobility shines even more brightly if ever it is seen.

Max: I see.

Homer: This brings us back to our original question.

Max: What question is that?

Homer: When an agent feels a moral obligation to do something in spite of the fact that it will in no way serve any particular interest of his, is such a feeling an illusion or is it real? That is, is it rational or irrational for him to feel bound by the moral law, even though what the moral law requires is contrary to the agent's strongest interest? In order to answer this question, we must consider it from the two different points of view.

Max: How is that?

Homer: If you consider the question strictly from the purely subjective point of view, without considering the objective point of view at all, it seems clearly an illusion to feel obligated under such conditions. For without considering the objective point of view, it seems as if doing what is moral in such situations can in no way contribute to the quality of one's consciously lived experience. Looking at the matter this way, reason must vote against doing what is moral.

Max: That certainly sounds right to me.

Moral action irrational from subj. point of view

Objectively, moral life is rational

NB. Hasn't H simply substituted "obj. point of view" for "moral point of view"? If so, he seems to be firmly within moral ballpark. What happens to relations? We seem to have lot right of it.

50   Part III

Homer: On the other hand, if you consider the matter from the purely objective point of view, without any consideration for the subjective point of view, then reason must reach the opposite conclusion. For, objectively speaking, the most honorable and praiseworthy life is without a doubt the moral life. Of that I have not the slightest doubt. For it is the moral person who gives the highest and most precious gift to society, the gift that makes society itself possible.

Max: But as you yourself pointed out, both of these perspectives are inescapable and inevitable for all rational animals such as ourselves. How, therefore, is reason to decide between these two conflicting verdicts? How can it bring them into a rational equilibrium?

Homer: By seeing that the verdict of reason from the purely objective point of view must prevail over the verdict of reason from the purely subjective point of view.

Max: And how might that be seen?

Homer: By seeing that there is a certain vital relationship between these two viewpoints, when they exist side by side as they do in each of us.

Max: And what relationship might that be?

Homer: Unless we satisfy the demands made upon us from the objective perspective, we will never really satisfy the demands made upon us from the subjective perspective either, for the first is a necessary condition of the second. Or to put it in plainer language, we can never be truly happy unless we are also worthy of happiness, unless we are also moral. priority of morality

Max: And what leads you to believe this? vs our self-interest

Homer: Because real freedom—inner freedom—is possible only for those who do their best to live the moral life. The person who places happiness above honor—above morality—tries thereby to build a life upon the quicksands of subjective viewpoints as if happiness were the supremely important thing about one's entire existence. But private enjoyments and subjective satisfactions are at best uncertain, unpredictable, and transient and, at worst, full of great pain and profound suffering. When we draw our last breath, these transient satisfactions vanish without a trace, but a life anchored upon the solid shores of morality is another matter.

Max: How is that?

Homer: The moral person steps into the larger stream of humanity, with a solid hold on the neighboring banks. Such a person becomes a part of something larger, more enduring, and more inspiring than his own immediate, subjective state—something he is prepared to die for, if necessary. Inwardly, self-transcending concern frees one from the fears of frustration, pain, and extinction.

Max: It sounds as if you are now talking about a different sort of freedom than you talked about earlier, when you mentioned freedom as our ability to shape what we become through rational choice. Now you seem to be talking about freedom as being inwardly free from certain sorts of fears and anxieties.

Homer: That's right. But note that the first sort of freedom is a necessary condition of the second sort of freedom. For only if you can shape yourself through your rational choices, will it be possible for you to live the moral life and so be inwardly free. That is, freedom of the will is a necessary condition of inner or moral freedom.

Max: Yes, I can see that that is the case.

Homer: Returning to my original claim, then, my argument is that inner freedom is a necessary condition of enduring happiness, and morality or honor, in turn, is a necessary condition of inner freedom. Therefore, morality or honor is a necessary condition of true happiness.

Max: And what follows from this?

H argues that objective, moral viewpoint is more rational
(than a self-interested point of view?)

52   Part III

Homer: If I am right in arguing this way, then reason must favor its verdict from the purely objective point of view over its verdict from the purely subjective point of view, when both of these points of view must be taken into consideration, as with humans. It follows that it is always rational to do the moral thing so that our feeling of moral obligation, even in cases where being moral runs counter to our strongest interest, is quite real and not illusory. That is, the belief that we have a moral duty in such cases is itself quite rational.

Max: I am not sure how I feel about your proposal, Homer. You talk more like an absolutist than like a relativist.

Homer: That is probably because, unlike many relativists, I have not dismissed everything that absolutists say as empty talk. I have, instead, taken the questions they have raised and tried to respond to them from a relativist viewpoint. Their intuitions about the agent's feelings of moral obligation seem to me to be quite right. But I have tried to account for such feelings in a way that permits me to retain the insights of relativism at the same time.

Max: It is not clear to me from what you have said that you will be able to do this. I think that what you have just now said about moral obligation will ultimately compel you to embrace some form of absolutism.

Homer: What makes you think that?

Max: You have made moral obligation into something unconditional and independent of the individual's particular interests, and this I think will ultimately lead you to assume a single absolute morality as well.

Homer: I can see why you might think that way, Max, but I assure you I can escape making such an assumption very easily.

Max: How is that?

Homer: By distinguishing the claim that we have an absolute duty to always do what is moral from the claim that what is

Homer : 1. Rejects egoism, moral scepticism, amoralism

2. But still maintains relativism. Morality is supremely important, but varies from one society to another

Homer's Ethical Relativism   53

moral is always a single and absolute thing. I believe we must always do what is moral, so I accept the first claim. But I believe that what is moral in one society is not the same as what is moral in another, so I reject the second claim. I reject that second claim, moreover, on essentially the same grounds as you do.

Max: You mean that you agree with my assumption that what is in the interests of society varies from society to society?

Homer: Yes. I differ from you only in saying that it is always rational to do what is moral, while you have denied this. For in my conception, to live the rational life is to live the worthy or meaningful life and to place honor or morality above everything else. It is to measure your life by what you give to the world and not in terms of what you take from it. Nonetheless, I accept your claim that what is in the true interests of a society will vary from society to society. And from this it follows, according to my reckoning, that what in fact is moral or honorable will vary from society to society. If infanticide or cannibalism are truly in the interests of some society, then I must agree with you that they are moral for that society. Of course, whether or not such practices ever are in the true interests of any society is another matter. It could be that such things have never really been in the interest of any society. But in case they are, then I would agree with you that they are moral. And in any case, I am quite convinced that what is in a people's true interest varies enormously from society to society and even for the same society from time to time. So you see I am every bit as much of a moral relativist as you are in spite of my claim that it is always rational for someone to do their moral duty—whatever that may be in any given case.

Max: I see. I must admit that in spite of your sounding very much like an absolutist when you explained the agent's moral obligation, you are indeed a bona fide moral relativist. From the look on Siddhartha's face, however, I am not sure that he entirely agrees with me on this matter. Am I reading you correctly, Siddhartha?

Reverts to an earlier arg: morality depends on what is in "true interest" of society. This varies between societies

Siddhartha: It never occurred to me that I was so transparent, but perhaps I am. For I must say I feel less certain than you seem to, Max, that Homer can have his cake and eat it too.

Max: Then perhaps I should let you take over the task of questioning Homer, Siddhartha, since I have nothing more to ask of him. And in any case, Siddhartha, it was our original plan to have you question each of us, since you are the only one among us to represent the absolutist point of view.

Homer: Max has a point, Siddhartha, and in any case I would like to know what your concerns are.

Siddhartha: When I said you wanted to have your cake and eat it too, Homer, I was referring to your partial acceptance of the absolutist position. On the one hand, you want to agree with the absolutist's contention that we have an absolute obligation to do what is moral, while on the other hand you want to claim that what is moral is nonetheless relative to a given society. I am not certain this can be done.

Homer: In your estimation, where do you think I go wrong?

Siddhartha: Your analysis of the two points of view, the subjective and the objective, is very useful and insightful, and I agree with almost everything you have said on these matters. However, I believe it would be useful to consider the objective or moral point of view a bit further.

Homer: What do you have in mind?

Siddhartha: I have in mind your notion of being worthy or honorable. I would like to examine that more closely.

Homer: I will do my best to help you all I can.

Siddhartha: Tell me then: Would you say that it is rational or irrational to do the honorable thing?

Homer: Given my understanding of honor, I would have to say it is always rational and never irrational to do the honorable thing.

Siddhartha: Granting that honor is something rational, it would seem we can be mistaken about that which constitutes true honor, for it is clear that we can be mistaken about what is truly rational.

Homer: I cannot deny that.

Siddhartha: Then tell me, Homer, would you say the happy slave—the slave who thinks it is honorable to serve his master— is mistaken about honor or not?

Homer: What do you mean?

Siddhartha: I am referring to a slave who has accepted the moral and legal norms of his master, who has chosen to think of himself as a member of the master's society, and who believes it is honorable to do his master's bidding, for example, to report on his fellow slaves when they act in ways that don't conform to his master's wishes. Would you say that such a slave's notion of honor is correct or mistaken?

Homer: I would want to consider this matter with some care before I answer.

Siddhartha: Then consider the matter from the perspective of rationality. Given the choice between being free or being someone's slave, which would you say is more rational?

Homer: It must be more rational to choose to be free. For to give up your freedom is to give up your right to make your own choices and so virtually to give up the exercise of your own rationality. And I cannot see how it would ever be rational to abandon rationality.

Siddhartha: Nor I, Homer. So do you now see how to answer my question about the happy slave's notion of honor?

Homer: I certainly do. I think we must say it is irrational for him to accept his master's values for his own and to regard his condition of slavery as an honorable one. Since it is irrational for the slave to be loyal to a slave-owner society in the first place, his notion of honor is irrational and therefore mistaken.

Siddhartha: Good. Indeed, we can say in general that honor is only real or genuine, if, in the first place, the choice to belong to the society in question was a rational choice.

Homer: I agree entirely.

Siddhartha: Let us inquire about the slave-owner himself then. Let us consider whether his honor is rational or real or not.

Homer: How do you propose to do that?

Siddhartha: By asking where, if the slave-owner has any honor at all, it might be located.

Homer: That sounds like a good plan to me. In my view, the slave-owner's honor is derived from his doing what best serves the interests of the society of which he is a member.

Siddhartha: Then let us ask ourselves, why is it that people regard it as honorable or noble to serve one's community in this way? Why is someone who will lay down his life for others honorable or noble, but not the person who selfishly clings to his own life and happiness?

Homer: Because the honorable person has risen above the narrow confines of a selfish existence and has worked for the happiness and welfare of others. Communities everywhere see this as noble or honorable.

Siddhartha: That is true, Homer. But tell me something regarding the slave-owner: Why is his nobility confined to merely serving the interests of his fellow slave-owners? Why doesn't he serve the interests of the slaves equally as well? Why has he so little regard for their happiness and their honor?

Homer: I think that you would find that the slave-owning class does not consider slaves as equals and believes they are suited for nothing better than being slaves.

Current societies (eg. slave-owning) are simply mistaken about the
nature of moral goodness, even acc. to the "objective" notion of
morality endorsed by H.

Siddhartha: But such beliefs are all of them blatant lies, are they not? For there is no instance of any race of humans, enslaved or not, that are without reason and so unfit to pursue a free and rational existence. Do you agree?

Homer: I certainly do. The Jews were once slaves and look at all the great things they have accomplished. Moreover, I can see equally great things coming from the Afro-Americans who were slaves only a hundred or so years ago.

Siddhartha: Let us note, moreover, that slavery has always served the interests of the slave-owners and no one else, Homer.

Homer: I can scarcely deny a thing so obvious.

Siddhartha: Well then, let us put these two things together— the blatant lies told by the slave-owners, and the serving of their own selfish interests. Can there be any doubt how they came to believe such lies, that it was not for any good reason but simply for self-serving interests that they held such beliefs in the first place? Did they not deceive themselves out of selfish interests?

Homer: I see that you are right about this as well, Siddhartha.

Siddhartha: Good. Then I think you will also agree that what they called honor was not genuine honor at all. For didn't we say just a moment ago that people call their heroes honorable because they have risen above the narrow confines of a selfish existence and have worked for the happiness and welfare of others?

Homer: We did.

Siddhartha: Yet as it turns out, the slave-owner is anything but honorable in his treatment of slaves. And even when he works for the good of the slave society, he is trying to preserve a way of life that entails both the dishonor of the slave and the slave-owner and so is a dishonorable way of life. So indeed, there can be no honor in that either.

Homer: Again I can't deny what you say.

Siddhartha: Then, I shall simply add that your troubles all stem
from trying to combine relativism and honor in the way you
have. I believe that in the final analysis you are going to find that
you can't sensibly hold fast to both of these, that you are going
to have to give up one or the other. If true honor exists at all,
Homer, it must be a single thing and not many things as moral
relativism implies.

S: if one concedes that there are genuine moral values (eg,
honor), then relativism is untenable. If there are genuine values,
then moral mistakes must be possible; but relativism cannot explain/
allow for the concept of a moral mistake.

Part IV

Siddhartha's Absolutist
Position Stated

Homer: You have, indeed, given me much food for thought, Siddhartha. However, it is now your turn. We would all like to hear your absolutist version of morality. It is time for us to question you as you have questioned each of us.

Siddhartha: Fair enough. Let me begin where we have just left off, with the matter of honor.

Homer: Good.

Siddhartha: In my view, there is but one community or society—the society of humans or persons. For, as we have noted, all persons are endowed with an ability to reason and so to pursue happiness and honor, which as you have noted, Homer, are universally necessary for everyone. It is this universal necessity that is essential to our nature, morally speaking, and that unites us as a true society. The division of various groups of people according to race, religion, nation, tribe, or what have you are all, in my view, arbitrary and artificial, and ultimately founded upon nothing but selfish interests, no matter how vehemently members of a particular society may proclaim their unique superiority. And the same goes for all of the divisions within such societies such as castes, classes, or special organizations, for they likewise are based upon arbitrary and artificial

59

criteria that are motivated only by greed and selfishness, and not upon sound argument or solid reasoning. These false notions of honor are, at best, severely incomplete and distorted. For genuine honor breaks free of the shackles of selfish longings and is guided by reason and by the recognition that the same longing for happiness and honor in one's own breast is equally present in everyone else's breast as well. It is impossible to do this and not at the same time see that there is but a single society, the society of persons, and that true honor lies in doing what is best, not for that society as a whole, but for the whole of that society—which is to say, to act in a way that reflects an equal regard for the happiness and honor of everyone.

Homer: That all sounds quite beautiful and noble, Siddhartha. I grant you that. It certainly evokes responsive chords in me at least. All the same, it is my duty to seek out any problems I see, for we must settle for nothing less than genuine honor. And sentiments, no matter how noble-sounding, are worth nothing if they lack a firm grounding in reality.

Siddhartha: I agree with you entirely, Homer. What is noble-sounding may turn out to be something else, just as what is human-sounding may not be human at all. Yet don't forget that just as it is true that what is human-sounding sometimes is human, so too what is noble-sounding sometimes really is noble. So in the first place keep in mind that what strikes a chord in us is sometimes a clue and is to be trusted. Moreover, there can be a certain justification in numbers. If something sounds human to most people or to everyone in a position to hear it clearly, that frequently means there is more reason to trust it as an indication of something human. And similarly, if something sounds noble to most people or to everyone in a position to hear it clearly, then that too may be taken as a partial reason to believe it really is noble. So, if what I have said sounds noble to you, Homer, and moreover would sound noble to most people or to everyone in a position to hear it clearly, then we already have some reason to believe it is noble from the start.

Homer: I accept what you say, Siddhartha. But as you know, people can be fooled, even most or all of them, sometimes. So granted we have some initial reasons for what you say, what further reasons can you give?

Siddhartha: A while ago you admitted there is no honor in being either a slave or a slave-owner, that on the one hand it would be irrational to choose slavery over freedom, while on the other it is really out of selfishness and not honor that slave-owners protect the interests of their society.

Homer: I found I could not deny this.

Siddhartha: Then I say to you, Homer, that what is true of slave and slave-owner is true in any other case where one group of people treats the members of some other group or any outsider with less regard than they have for those within their group. You cannot tell me it would be rational or honorable for those who receive inferior treatment to accept being treated that way. Nor, therefore, can you tell me it is honorable for the group that thinks itself superior to them to treat them as if they were inferior. For to treat others that way is to treat them in a way they could not rationally will themselves to be treated and therefore is contrary to their own honor. There can be no honor in treating people in such a way, for it is based upon arbitrary distinctions that are motivated only by selfishness and not by good reasoning or by anything noble or honorable.

Homer: That is helpful, Siddhartha. But I am now concerned about what all of this means when we get down to cases, or how it translates into some sort of morality.

Siddhartha: Then let me come at the problem from an entirely fresh angle. Let us begin by reflecting upon self-love, what it is, and what it implies.

Homer: I am with you.

Siddhartha: Would you say that someone who had unhealthy living habits, drank excessively, and gambled away all his earnings loved himself or not?

Homer: I would say that he did not love himself, since he is doing things that will make him unhappy. Self-love prompts a person to act in ways that promote his happiness, not destroy it.

Siddhartha: And what would you say of someone who hated himself and saw nothing good in himself? Would you say he loves himself or not?

Homer: It is only too obvious that to the extent you hate yourself and feel you are useless, you don't love yourself.

Siddhartha: And how would you explain this phenomenon of hating yourself or not accepting yourself, and of not thinking there is anything good about yourself or failing to appreciate yourself?

Homer: A failure to accept ourselves arises from a knowledge of our faults and blemishes and an inability to see that we are still worthy in spite of these imperfections. Some people fret about their physical appearance or health, others about their lack of artistry or musical abilities, and still others about their age or lack of worldly success. A failure to appreciate ourselves, on the other hand, arises because we don't see all of our good points and strengths and our wonderful potentials. Each person is, after all, a unique combination of positive qualities, if only one can look for them and see them. I have seen people who were endowed with very little turn their lives into beautiful models for us all; others who had everything became consumed with envy and jealousy and so completely overlooked their own natural gifts.

Siddhartha: So a person who can truly be said to love himself will not only seek to promote his own happiness, but will accept and appreciate himself for what he is as well. Now let me ask you about young people when they reach a certain stage of development. Some reach it sooner than others, but it most frequently seems to occur somewhere between the ages fourteen to twenty. Have you ever noted how they want to do everything on their own and rebel against their parents' authority and advice?

Homer: How could I have failed to note it, Siddhartha. I went through all of that myself, as I am sure you have.

Siddhartha: Yes. And would you say it is a healthy thing or not?

Homer: Speaking for myself, I'd have to say it was mixed, both healthy and not healthy. On the one hand, it led me to do some foolish things simply because I was too proud to benefit from my parents' greater experience. On the other hand, I had to learn to think for myself and to make my own choices, even if I sometimes made some mistakes.

Siddhartha: It is frequently a hard time for everyone, parent and child alike. But wise parents who understand this fundamental human need to be our own decision-makers can make matters easier by gradually allowing their children more and more control of their own lives as they demonstrate a reasonable ability to do so. Wise and loving parents see that they must balance their concern for their children with a respect for their children's powerful need for autonomy. For without autonomy, no one can feel worthy or honorable. You yourself have clearly shown autonomy to be necessary to be fully human. So the need for autonomy is itself healthy, and it is just a matter of the parents making certain that the youngsters do not assume more decision-making responsibility than they are ready to handle at any given time. Wise and loving parents will respect their youngsters need for autonomy and carefully balance that against their own protective urges.

Homer: I certainly agree with that.

Siddhartha: Then I think we can also say that someone who does not respect his or her own autonomy does not fully love himself or herself either, that self-love also entails a certain respect for one's own autonomy.

Homer: I would have to agree with that too.

Siddhartha: Since respecting our own autonomy is such an important part of self-love, Homer, let us consider it with some care, by inquiring just where our autonomy lies.

Homer: Well, it consists in making our own decisions about our own lives. That much we have already established. So it implies our working out our happiness and honor for ourselves without outside interference.

Siddhartha: It means that much to be sure. But tell me what you would say of someone who is ignorant, who had no understanding of happiness or honor, and who was in every way irrational. Would you say she had much freedom or autonomy simply because she made her own decisions?

Homer: I would say that she is the least free or autonomous of all, for she is clearly ruled by the childish element in herself.

Siddhartha: So would you agree that the truly free or autonomous person is enlightened about true happiness and honor and is ruled by the rational element in her psyche?

Homer: I would agree entirely.

Siddhartha: Then I think you will agree that while the truly free or autonomous person will always decide matters for herself, she is nonetheless eager to learn from others by seeking their advice and insight. For she is forever eager to be more and more enlightened about matters concerning happiness and honor and to be ruled by reason.

Homer: That is very true. And this is no doubt why most youngsters eventually come to appreciate their parents and are eager to learn from them and from others as well once they have passed through the rebellious stage and are secure in their ability to make their own decisions.

Siddhartha: Then I believe it is fair to say that someone who

really respects his own autonomy or freedom, in the end, respects his ability to reason and the importance of developing it
and letting it govern his decision-making. We might therefore
say that to respect our autonomy—which is implied by self-
love—is, in the end, to respect the rule of reason in ourselves.

Homer: I accept what you say.

Siddhartha: Now tell me, Homer, do you see a connection
between what is generally called autonomy—the thing that is so
important to young people—and what you earlier referred to as
inner freedom?

Homer: I certainly do. For they are, in fact, the very same
thing. In both cases we are talking about a person's exercising
her own reason to come to a decision. It is being governed by
honor, reason, and insight, rather than by other people, fear,
and ignorance. The free person is the only one who is truly her
own person. And to be free means to be rational and honorable,
and inwardly free of fear.

Siddhartha: You have said exactly what I'd hoped you'd say.
And I think we might add that only the rational and honorable
person is truly in command of herself. She alone has her priorities well ordered and knows how much weight to give to her
various desires and interests. She alone has mastered herself
and her life.

Homer: I would be the last to deny that.

Siddhartha: And she alone has true courage. Her courage is
not like the false courage of the bully who is brave only when
his or her strength is superior. Nor is it like the courage of the
fool whose courage is the result of ignorance of what is really to
be feared. Rather she is courageous even in the face of those
who have greater power or strength than herself and has fear
only when she ought to, and not otherwise. For she knows that,
as Plato said, the only thing that is really to be feared is to do a
dishonorable or immoral deed. Thus, her courage is based upon
knowing what is and what is not really to be feared. And in
knowing this, she is truly, inwardly free.

Homer: That is my own view of the matter, Siddhartha.

Siddhartha: Good. Then we can add that the person who truly loves herself values her autonomy, and this implies a love of honor or morality that makes her her own master and truly courageous and therefore inwardly free.

Homer: I accept all that you say.

Siddhartha: Then I think we ought to amend slightly what you said earlier.

Homer: Why is that?

Siddhartha: Earlier you said that morality is a necessary condition of happiness.

Homer: I did.

Siddhartha: On considering the matter, I think that you should have said more than this. Morality or honor is not simply a necessary condition of happiness, but a sufficient condition of happiness.

Homer: I was inclined to say the same thing, but backed off from going that far. For it seemed to me I might be claiming too much in saying such a thing.

Siddhartha: I understand your reluctance, Homer. It is indeed a bold thing to say. Yet, I believe it is quite true when morality is fully comprehended and practiced. For those who fully comprehend and practice the right morality are not partially, but completely free inwardly. And that complete inner freedom, Homer, is what I call true happiness.

Homer: I must say that I am highly sympathetic with your stronger position on this matter, but I still have to admit to some uncertainty. I will have to give all of this a lot more thought. In the meantime, you have not explained morality in terms of self-love as you promised you would. So I must now ask you to keep your word, Siddhartha, or lose your honor.

Siddhartha: Well said, Homer. You are right to scold me and get me back on track. But my digression was not without purpose. For now that we have examined the nature of self-love with some care, it will be relatively easy to explain my conception of morality and of honor to you. For myself, the whole of morality may be stated in these simple words: Treat others as you would, out of self-love, have others treat you.

Homer: Unless I am mistaken, Siddhartha, you have simply stated the Golden Rule in slightly different words.

Siddhartha: You are not in the least mistaken, Homer. I think that the famous words "Do unto others as you would have them do unto you," if understood in terms of the sort of rational or ideal self-love we have discussed above, captures the 'a' through the 'z' of all morality.

Homer: I have an idea of what you have in mind, but I would like to see you spell it out in more detail if you would.

Siddhartha: Self-love, we have agreed, entails caring for one's own happiness, an acceptance of one's limitations, and an appreciation of one's unique assets and potentials, a respect for one's autonomy or reason, and, above all, a concern for one's honor. Now consider what this implies concerning how, out of self-love, you would have others treat you. Out of self-love you would not have others be indifferent to your concern for happiness; you would have them help you if you need help and they are able to help. Nor would you have others demean or ridicule you, or reject you because of your imperfections, or fail to acknowledge and appreciate your assets and potentials. And, moreover, out of respect for your autonomy, you would have them help you only when you really need help, respect your wishes when you don't require advice, and also respect your need to make the final decisions on your own regarding the management of your life. Finally, and above all, out of your concern for your honor, you would want others to never do anything that might in some way undermine your capacity or determination to do what is moral or honorable.

Summary of ethic of self-love, & what it demands of others toward you

Homer: I see. Then to treat others in the same way I would, out of self-love, be treated is simply to treat them in all the ways you have just now mentioned. Is that it?

Siddhartha: That's it exactly. If you followed the Golden Rule properly, then the very same concern you would have others show for your happiness, you would likewise show for the happiness of others. The very same acceptance of your imperfections and appreciation of your good qualities and potentials you would want from others, you would give to them. The very same respect you demand for your autonomy or freedom, you would have for the freedom or autonomy of others. And just as you would, out of rational self-love, have no one undermine your honor, you would never do anything to undermine the honor of another.

Homer: And how can that guide us when we are considering the moral or legal norms of some society?

Siddhartha: We must always evaluate the legal and moral practices of any society according to the Golden Rule. They are genuinely moral only so far as they satisfy that rule.

Homer: I see. So long as a law or moral norm is consistent with everyone's self-love, it is truly moral. But if it is inconsistent with the self-love of one or more persons, then it is, in truth, an immoral law or norm. So when it is said everyone is equal before the law or that the truly moral order treats everyone as an equal, you would say this means everyone's self-love must be given an equal importance or regard. ˄ Summary (by H) of S; basic moral principle, based on equal respect for everyone's self-love

Siddhartha: Yes.

Homer: Well, I see a problem with this.

Siddhartha: What is that?

Homer: There are times when two or more parties' interests, welfare, or happiness conflict. What serves one will work against the other and vice versa. These no-win situations make it impossible to have an equal regard for the self-love of both parties

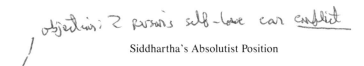

involved in the conflict and, therefore, impossible to do what is moral, according to you.

Siddhartha: Those are situations calling for agonizing choices to be sure, but whether they admit of morally right choices is another matter. Give me a specific example so that we can think it through together.

Homer: Let us imagine that we are on an island and that among us are twenty people urgently requiring immediate medical attention. However, we only have one boat to take people to the mainland—a two day's journey roundtrip—and the boat will only hold five sick people at a time. How could you resolve such a problem in a way that is consistent with everyone's self-love?

Siddhartha: Let us take matters a step at a time. First of all, out of self-love all twenty would agree that it is better to take some than none.

Homer: That is obvious since everyone would lose if no action were taken.

Siddhartha: And all would out of self-love also see that all can't pile into the boat since again all would lose on that account, and that a reasonable limit must be agreed upon—which you have assumed to be five each trip, if we further suppose no other boats are available on the mainland. And so they would all agree, since we assume they are rational and honorable if they are truly self-loving, that some method of selection is necessary and that it should be one reflecting an equal regard for everyone's self-love.

Homer: I can see how all of that follows from what you have said earlier about rational or ideal self-love, Siddhartha.

Siddhartha: Good. Then let me ask you this. Would you say a doctor has shown an equal regard for two patients' self-love, if he treats them on the basis of first-come, first-served, without any consideration for the degree or seriousness of their illness?

Homer: Certainly not. For if one has only a simple cold but the other is about to die unless treated immediately, the doctor would not be showing the dying person an equal consideration, if he took the patient with a cough first, simply because of the first-come, first-served rule.

Siddhartha: I take it in that case that you will then agree with me that the very first thing that must be done in applying the Golden Rule to the situation you mentioned must be to determine which patients are in greatest need in getting to the mainland first.

Homer: I could not say otherwise.

Siddhartha: Then let us call all considerations such as these, where an equal regard for each person's self-love leads to fair but differential treatment, nonrandom considerations. I think you will agree that such considerations are quite consistent with each person's self-love.

Homer: I do.

Siddhartha: Let us then assume that all such nonrandom considerations, such as the degree of illness, have been exhausted and that there are still fifteen people remaining. Assume these fifteen people are equally ill and that we cannot decide who shall go in what order in any nonrandom way that is consistent with each person's self-love. In that case, the remaining fifteen will, out of a rational self-love, see that there is no alternative but to find an utterly random means of selection that gives everyone an equal chance. For that is what must now be done to show an equal regard for everyone's self-love. Drawing lots, a throw of the die, choosing cards, or any such procedure would do, so long as it is entirely random.

Homer: So when we are considering the laws of the land or its moral norms, we shall have to engage in a similar balancing act, taking the greatest care we know how to see that they are consistent with everyone's self-love.

S's recognition of human fallibility does not undermine
his belief in absolute nature of moral obligation
Siddhartha's Absolutist Position   71

Siddhartha: That's right. In principle, every single person must be considered, every last soul. Our eyes should miss no one. And every aspect of their self-love, their autonomy and honor as well as their happiness, must be given its due consideration.

Homer: But that is impossible, Siddhartha.

Siddhartha: For fools such as us, Homer, you are perfectly right. In practice, there is no way mere humans such as ourselves can ever hope to comprehend everyone's situation, or how the laws or moral norms of the land will affect them, nor just how consistent they will be with everyone's self-love. Still we must try to do our very best, knowing we will never succeed perfectly. And that is why, if we really wish to be moral in our dealings with people, we must not insist upon the absolute letter of even basically just laws, for they are, at best, the crude and fallible instruments of mere men such as ourselves. It has been said that we must follow the spirit of the law and that, rightly understood, always means the Golden Rule, as I have just explained. And even in following this rule, we cannot but err, for the realities of moral life are enormously complex and can never be understood completely.

Homer: So the matter is in a way hopeless, Siddhartha. A while ago you said honor is something within our reach. But now if I understand you, it will often be just a bit beyond us since it depends upon doing what is moral, and you have just now admitted we can't know with exactness what is moral.

Siddhartha: There is a paradox here, Homer, but not a contradiction. Indeed, let me add that I think we are sometimes bound to fail to do what is moral not only because we lack the proper understanding, but because we sometimes lack the will—something even more serious as far as our honor is concerned. Nonetheless, we must strive to do the best we can. We must forgive ourselves, forgive others, and ask them to forgive us for our failures. There is no alternative to this.

Homer: How do you see that?

Siddhartha: Self-love requires it, since self-love implies self-acceptance, and that in turn entails self-forgiveness.

Homer: But I see a danger here. Honor requires a certain sternness, a taking oneself in hand for past misdeeds and not permitting any softness on the matter.

Siddhartha: The opposite is true as I see it. It is not with respect to past deeds that we must be stern and take ourselves in hand, but with respect to present and future deeds. For to look so harshly to our past deeds in that way is to make a fetish out of honor.

Homer: But I thought you said honor was the surest and highest form of freedom.

Siddhartha: That is quite true, Homer. But being honorable and being anxious about *our* honor are not the same thing. To be truly honorable is to love your neighbor as yourself, to treat others in the way you, out of self-love, would be treated. So the truly honorable person's gaze is upon doing what is consistent with everyone's self-love first and only derivatively upon their own honor. People who are always focusing upon how honorable *they* are are very prideful and not truly honorable at all. The loving spirit, which is the basis of all true honor, focuses creatively upon the present and future and not destructively upon the past. It keeps guilt from becoming a morbid self-preoccupation by creatively transforming it into present and future acts of love.

Homer: I think I see what you mean, Siddhartha. Our concern should always be with being honorable in the present and in the future, and this you wish to say is something different from our concern with how honorable we may or may not have been in the past. For the former leads us to concentrate upon doing what is consistent with everyone's self-love, while the latter leads us to concentrate only upon ourselves as if we are the most important thing in the world and that is the very opposite of true honor. *(eg. Williams)*

NB. A good response to the objection that moral integrity is a selfish concept

Siddhartha: That is it exactly. For a concentration upon past deeds, if they were unworthy, causes us to hate ourselves and to underestimate our present and future potential for good. While, if our deeds were worthy, it leads to pride, which is to say, the vain illusion that we are better than others, and this in turn blinds us to the merits of others as well as to our own real failings. And finally, the focusing upon the past misdeeds of others in unforgiving ways leads us to judge them and to thirst for their blood, which is certainly not consistent with their self-love or with genuine morality or honor. We must, therefore, accept human frailty, even in matters of honor, whether in ourselves or in others, lest we bring an even greater dishonor upon ourselves and others as well.

Homer: So in your view, self-love and love of others entails forgiveness for past misdeeds. Are you saying that people should never be held responsible for what they do?

Siddhartha: Not at all. To forgive yourself or another for wrongdoing implies responsibility. You can't forgive where there is no responsibility.

Homer: But what about punishment? Is that compatible with forgiveness?

Siddhartha: Forgiveness rules out punishment as vengeance, but it does not rule out the possibility of other reasons for punishment, for example, deterrence or rehabilitation. However, the arguments in favor of punishment are not very convincing, and I think that people who enthusiastically advocate punishment are actually thirsty for blood. Nonetheless, punishment is a grey area, as far as I can see, for there may be reasons for punishment that are consistent with everyone's self-love, including the person punished.

Homer: In your view then, Siddhartha, there is but a single principle by which any moral norm or law or action can be judged, the principle that every last person is to be treated in a way that is consistent with his or her own self-love. Or, in other

S advocates holding people responsible for past misdeeds, but readily forgiving them. He then asserts a very implausible, purely util concept of punishment. (He rules out retribution)

words, each person is always to live and act in a way that is consistent with everyone's self-love. A person's self-love, in turn, entails a concern for her own happiness, respect for her autonomy that includes a concern for her honor, and a basic acceptance and appreciation of herself that entails forgiveness.

Siddhartha: That's right, Homer. If something is consistent with everyone's self-love, then it is morally permissible, while if the absence of that thing is inconsistent with everyone's self-love, then it is morally obligatory. It is my view that consistency with everyone's self-love is the supreme and absolute principle of all true morality. A person is truly honorable to the extent he lives by this principle.

Homer: I can see clearly now why you think honor leads you to absolutism and why you say it is incompatible with relativism. And I assure you that if it comes to a parting of the ways, as you believe it must, I would sooner stay with honor than with relativism. Still, I will need to consider the matter much more carefully before I am as fully convinced as you are that honor and relativism are irreconcilable, that there is but one single, true honor.

Siddhartha: I do not blame you, Homer. For the matters we are discussing are too important to decide until you have ample time to consider them on your own.

S seems to base his case for moral absolutism on a simplistic, debatable moral theory, i.e. a 'self love' spin on Kant's ends in themselves & universalizability principles. It is surely a mistake to make moral absolutism hinge on the truth of any particular moral theory. Or perhaps S's point is simply that here is one clear eg. of an plausible absolute moral theory - there are many others.

Part V

Dilemma's and Max's Attacks on Siddhartha's Views

Homer: For the moment, I have no further questions, but I would like to hear what Dilemma and Max have to say about your views, Siddhartha.

Max: I need time to formulate my questions. Why don't you go first, Dilemma? You seem to have a ready question.

Dilemma: I do. I would like to pursue my original concern over being scientific. The philosopher Gilbert Harman has recently made some interesting observations about the absolutist-relativist debate. Harman has suggested that if you insist that, above all else, morality must fit into the world of facts revealed by science, moral relativism, or perhaps noncognitivism or skepticism, is likely to seem right. On the other hand, if you insist that, above all else, ethics must accord with our firmest and deepest prescientific beliefs and feelings about right and wrong, then you are more likely to be an absolutist. I believe that what really distinguishes Max and me from you, and perhaps from Homer as well, is the importance we place upon being scientific in dealing with ethics. Max and I, and Harman as well, hold that it is science or nothing. The demands of science must come first, those of ethics second. You and Homer seem to hold that it is ethics in accord with your prescientific intuitions, or nothing. If science can't understand such ethics "so much the worse for

Science rules out moral realism

75

science" seems to express your attitude. Do you agree with my assessment of the differences between us?

Siddhartha: In part, I do. There is no denying that, when it comes to the values I choose to live by, an ethics that satisfies my deepest, most persistent beliefs and feelings comes first, science second. And I can see that for you and Max, it is the other way around. I also can see that it is your overriding desire to be scientific that leads you and Max to find relativism more attractive than absolutism. And finally, I admit that above all else it is my loyalty to my firmest and deepest, prescientific beliefs and feelings about what is right and wrong that has led me to an ethic of love as the single true morality. However, I would like to make a distinction that neither you nor Harman seem to make.

Dilemma: And what is that?

Siddhartha: It is one thing to say that out of a desire to be scientific, you *in fact do* find relativism more attractive than absolutism and quite another to say that out of a desire to be scientific you *rationally ought to* find relativism more attractive than absolutism. I accept that the former is true of you and Harman and of many others, but I emphatically deny that the latter is true at all. I believe that this widespread belief that relativism is somehow more scientific than absolutism rests upon a mistake.

Dilemma: I would have thought you'd have found it obvious that, from a strictly scientific point of view, relativism is the logical choice.

Siddhartha: Then let me ask you something. A while back when Max and I agreed that the word 'moral' has more than one sense, did you agree with us on this point?

Dilemma: I must say that I listened to your arguments with great interest, Siddhartha, and I agreed that there must be a second sense of the word 'moral', just as you insisted.

Siddhartha: And do you agree that, in the first of these senses, the word 'moral' means roughly 'that which conforms to the moral norms of some society'?

Dilemma: I do.

Siddhartha: Would you further agree that it is not the first sense just mentioned, but some second sense that is the really important sense? That it is the second sense that people ordinarily argue about and take seriously when they are trying to decide what to do?

Dilemma: I would.

Siddhartha: Well then my view on the matter is this: Although science has shown that what is moral in the first, unimportant sense is relative, it has done nothing whatever to show that what is moral in the second sense is also relative. I agree with Ruth Benedict and other anthropologists when they point out that what is *believed* to be moral varies from culture to culture. However, I deny their conclusion that it follows that what *is* moral varies from culture to culture. As G. E. Moore noted, you simply can't get an action-guiding 'ought' from a descriptive 'is'!

Dilemma: I accept what you say with qualifications. I agree with G. E. Moore that you can't get the 'ought' of morality from the 'is' of science. However, Harman's point is the different point that while a relativist interpretation of morals in the second sense is *compatible* with science, that is explainable scientifically, an absolutist interpretation is not. Hence, science favors relativism over absolutism.

Siddhartha: And upon what grounds does Harman argue this to be the case?

Dilemma: On the basis of his analysis of the notion of having a *sufficient reason* to do something. Consider a successful, professional criminal who has no qualms about harming, even killing, people who do not belong to his inner circle. Would you not insist that such a criminal is irrational, that he has a sufficient reason not to harm strangers no matter how he happens to view the matter or feel about it?

Siddhartha: I certainly would.

Dilemma: Indeed, as an absolutist you have no choice but to say that. For as an absolutist you must say that if even one person has a morally sufficient reason not to harm strangers in a given set of circumstances, then every person has a morally sufficient reason not to harm strangers in those same set of circumstances. But as a relativist, I am free to say of two persons in exactly the same set of circumstances, that while one does, the other does not have a morally sufficient reason not to harm some stranger. And I can explain this difference by referring to the differences between the societies they have chosen to belong to. Hence, I can say that the criminal has no such morally sufficient reason, but that you and I do have such a sufficient reason not to harm a stranger simply by referring to the different societies the criminal, you, and I have chosen to belong to. As an absolutist, you have to make sense out of saying that the criminal also has a sufficient reason not to harm others, and this I don't think you can do.

Siddhartha: Then you are forgetting the two lines of argument Homer and I considered just a while ago.

Dilemma: What two lines of argument do you have in mind?

Siddhartha: The first originated with Homer. Recall that Homer distinguished between two different points of view from which each of us, as rational animals, must view his or her life. To the extent that we are rational, we will consider our lives from both the subjective and the objective points of view, the first being a concern with our happiness and the second a concern with our morality or worthiness. Homer argued, moreover, that it is rational to place the demands of the objective perspective and so morality above the demands of the subjective perspective. I argued from that point that all that Homer had said committed him to the view that there is really only one society, the human society, and so only one, single morality—a morality equally concerned with and equally respectful of everyone. If all of this is correct, then indeed it is always rational for *everyone* to treat strangers with respect and to be concerned about their well-being. Hence, in any circumstance that I have a sufficient reason not to harm a stranger, so does the criminal, whether he realizes this or not.

Dilemma: But this is mere conjecture, not science.

Siddhartha: I agree that it is not science. But I see nothing in Homer's theory about the objective and subjective perspectives that is in any way "unscientific" or contrary to science. It may run contrary to certain *philosophies* of science. However, it does not run counter to any existing *science* I am aware of. Nor is it any more conjectural or any less scientific than the theories that you and Max have articulated.

Dilemma: What distinction do you have in mind when you contrast *science* and *philosophies* of science?

Siddhartha: Well, consider the difference between B. F. Skinner's behaviorism and his experimental work on pigeons. The latter entails a lot of useful observations about the behavior of lower animals and has resulted in the development of many interesting concepts, such as reinforcement and extinction, in the field of animal psychology. This is what I mean by science. And we may leave it to future scientists to assess the worth of such work. However, Skinner's behaviorism—particularly as it applies to human beings—is another matter. According to the principles subsumed under the label "behaviorism," humans have no free will. According to behaviorism, we can entirely ignore what goes on in people's minds in the study of human behavior. Indeed, Skinner assumes, without any solid experimental evidence, that humans are in no essential ways different from pigeons, that whatever basic concepts or principles suffice to understand pigeons suffice equally for understanding humans. Whatever you think about the truth of these claims, this is *philosophy* of science, not science.

a better distinction would be empirical science v. methodological or metaphysical questions

Dilemma: I see now what you mean when you distinguish science and the philosophy of science. But why do you insist that only the current philosophies of science and not science give support to relativism?

Siddhartha: Let me use Skinner's work again to illustrate my point. In his book *Beyond Freedom and Dignity,* Skinner rejects Moore's distinction between 'is' versus 'ought', or 'description' versus 'prescription'. His argument against this distinction, moreover, is based upon his claim that humans are not free to adopt or not adopt moral principles *rationally,* but are strictly indoctrinated by their culture to adopt this or that moral norm. From there, it is only a short step to his further conclusion that moral principles are culturally relative. Thus, we can see that Skinner's moral relativism follows from his philosophy, his behaviorism, and not from his science.

Dilemma: I think I now see what you mean: You are saying that what is true of Skinner is true of all of us who claim that only relativism and not absolutism is compatible with science.

Siddhartha: That's it exactly. There is nothing today that I would call "science" that compels us to deny that moral principles are transculturally or universally valid. Indeed, current *science* sheds very little light upon ethics at all. Current philosophies of science are another matter. They tend to reduce humans to some purely biological, behavioral, biochemical or other mechanistic category and so strip humans of the capacity for true rationality or of universally valid principles of ethics.

Dilemma: For the sake of argument I will concede your point, Siddhartha. I grant you that it is the current philosophies of science more than science that support relativism. Still that is hardly to be ignored. For it is the current developments in science that have inspired the current philosophies of science.

Siddhartha: I have no doubt that there is something in what you say. But only future developments in science itself can tell us how wise or foolish our current philosophies of science are,

Self-love, which is essential to well-being, requires the moral life. This is another answer to egoistic challenges

especially as they apply to the human sciences, which are at best at an infantile stage of development. Let us not forget that philosophers who were overly impressed with the theory of evolution propounded some very dangerous and very foolish social doctrines.

Dilemma: Then let us note our disagreement at this juncture and move on. What of the second line of argument you mentioned? Was that the line of argument arising from your analysis of self-love?

Siddhartha: That's right. It is really a parallel argument to the first. Self-love is simply valuing yourself in a way that is appropriate to what you are essentially. To love yourself or properly value yourself is to be concerned with your happiness, to respect your autonomy or inner freedom, and so value your honor or morality above all else. That's the part that coincides with Homer's notions about the objective and subjective perspectives. But self-acceptance, which includes self-forgiveness, and self-appreciation are additional aspects of self-love that Homer did not consider. From there I argued that genuine self-love, an appropriate valuing of the humanity in yourself, entails acting in a way that is consistent with everyone's self-love, in appropriately valuing the very same humanity that is in everyone else. If this is right, then here is another way of seeing why the criminal has a sufficient reason not to harm a stranger just as much as we do. For they, no less than we, are acting contrary to their own self-love whenever they disregard some stranger's self-love. Now I do not claim that science has provided grounds for these psychological assumptions. But I do deny that it provides any greater support for the psychological assumptions you and Max, or any other relativist, have assumed.

Dilemma: True, I can't point to any existing science that shows our psychological assumptions are more plausible than yours. However, I believe the future development of science will support our side.

Siddhartha: Then it would seem that where we really part company is not with respect to any existing *science*, but with

It's not clear how science or phil. sci. could prove or disprove S's ethical theory

respect to our *philosophies* of science and our predictions about a future science of psychology. You and Max predict the matter will settle in your favor. I predict the matter will never settle or that, if it does, it will settle in my favor. But that scarcely makes you and Max more scientific than I. For *science* as it actually exists can't be said to favor one view over the other.

Dilemma: Then let us agree to wait and see what the future will bring.

Siddhartha: On that we can certainly agree.

Dilemma: Then I am content to turn you over to Max, Siddhartha. Provided you are ready to take over, Max?

Max: I am ready. I would like to pick up where you left off, Dilemma.

Dilemma: Good. I will be interested to see what you have in mind.

Max: I have in mind the two lines of argument by which Siddhartha has defended his position.

Siddhartha: What are your concerns?

Max: Consider first the line of argument that builds upon Homer's views. For the sake of argument, let us suppose that Homer is right in arguing that the subjective and objective points of view are inescapable, and also that it is always rational to give priority to the objective point of view over the subjective point of view in cases where they lead to conflicting requirements. Let me grant you all of that. I still see a fatal flaw in your argument from that point to the conclusion that there is but a single society and therefore but a single, true ethics.

Siddhartha: I see, and just where does this fatal flaw lie?

Max: Unless I am mistaken you reasoned roughly as follows: Your first premise was that to be rational is to be moral on all occasions. Your second premise was that to be moral is to do

M challenges S's assertion that harming individuals is necessarily contrary to interests of society as a whole.

Attacks on Siddhartha's Views   83

whatever is in the best interests of society. And your third premise was that to disregard the interests of anyone is to disregard what is in the best interests of society. From this you drew the conclusion that to disregard the interests of anyone is immoral and so irrational. Now your first two premises are Homer's assumptions, and I shall not challenge them. But your third premise is your own assumption, and therein lies your fatal flaw as far as I am concerned. For I deny that it is always, or even generally, in the best interest of *a society as a whole* to have a regard for the interests of *the whole of society,* that is, to have a regard for the interests of everyone. In particular, although the slave-owner may be said to disregard the interests of the slave, he can hardly be said to disregard what is best for his society as a whole. For in fact it may be in the best interests of the vast majority, and so in the best interest of a society as a whole, to sacrifice some of its members by making them slaves. Therefore, I deny your claim that the slave-owner is necessarily acting only out of selfish motives rather than genuinely moral motives. For slave-owners may be said to be serving the best interests of their society as a whole.

Siddhartha: I can easily see how you have rejected my third premise, Max. It certainly does require further defense. However, before I respond to you, let me hear your objection to my second line of argument. For I may be able to respond to both objections at the same time.

Max: Very well. My objection to your second line of argument has to do with your claim that self-love entails the love of others, that if someone really loves himself he therefore will act in a way that is consistent with everyone's self-love. I will accept your claim that self-love entails self-concern, for one's own happiness, and self-respect, for one's own autonomy and honor or morality. That simply seems to be Homer's position restated. I will even accept your claim that self-love entails self-acceptance, and so self-forgiveness, as well as self-appreciation. What you have not shown, however, is the crucial point, namely that to be moral is to have a regard for the love each person ideally

Why has S allowed himself to get cornered into basing morality on the best interests of society? (a kind of util. on a national scale)

Again, why does he bring the interests of society into the picture?

84   Part V

or rationally has for himself. It is exactly at this point that you make a tremendous, unwarranted leap in your argument.

Siddhartha: As I suspected might be the case, your objections to my two lines of argument have turned out to be one and the same objection. For if it can be shown that self-love entails a love of all others, then it will follow that it is always in the best interests of any particular society as a whole to have a regard for the whole of society. If you agree with me on this, then we can focus upon self-love and consider why I am so certain it necessarily entails the love of everyone.

Max: That sounds fine to me.

Siddhartha: Then let us begin by noting where we are in agreement with one another. We agree that to be moral, and so rational, entails doing what is in the best interests of society as a whole. Am I correct about this?

Max: I have granted you that much for the sake of argument, since that is Homer's view.

Siddhartha: In that case, I believe you must also grant me that doing what is moral, and so rational, also entails doing what is consistent with the self-love of the majority of the members of your own society. For surely, it cannot be in the best interests of a society as a whole to act in any way that is contrary to the self-love of the majority of its members. Do you agree to this as well?

Max: It would seem to follow from what we have already agreed upon.

Siddhartha: Then let us pinpoint our disagreement as follows: While you say that being moral, and so rational, only entails acting in a way that is consistent with the self-love of the majority of members of your own society, I hold that being moral, and so rational, entails acting in a way that is consistent with the self-love of absolutely every person, no matter what society they belong to or even if they should happen to belong to no society at all. Would you agree that that is a fair character-ization of our present disagreement?

Max: I would.

Siddhartha: Then let us examine with greater care just what is involved in acting in a way that is consistent with another's self-love. Let us imagine what it would be like for another to act in a way that is consistent with your self-love, Max. Does that sound like an agreeable plan?

Max: It does.

Siddhartha: We have agreed that out of self-love you would will others to take account of your happiness, autonomy, and honor. And you would also will that they accept and appreciate you just as you accept and appreciate yourself. Is that correct?

Max: It is.

Siddhartha: Now we may ask just how far you would out of self-love expect them to take account of your happiness, auton-omy, and honor.

Max: What do you mean?

Siddhartha: Under what conditions would you out of self-love will that they take account of your happiness, for example?

Max: Under all conditions where what they do would have a bearing upon my happiness, naturally.

Siddhartha: And the same would apply to your honor and your autonomy as well, I suppose? And also to their accepting and appreciating you?

Max: Certainly.

Siddhartha: In short, out of a rational self-love, you would never have another totally disregard these things whenever what they might do could have a significant effect upon one or more of these things. That much at least is implied by the notion of

S tries to rule out scapegoat cases by appeal to ends in themselves type principle / appeal to individual rights

another acting in a way that is consistent with your self-love, is it not?

Max: Yes.

Siddhartha: So to act in a way that is consistent with some one person's rational self-love is to do so *unconditionally* and not just sometimes or under certain conditions.

Max: That would seem to follow from all we have agreed upon so far.

Siddhartha: Now tell me, Max, how does it feel to be totally disregarded by another?

Max: It evokes in me the strongest feelings of indignation you can imagine.

Siddhartha: You are no different from other people on this score. Just ask any woman who has been raped, anyone who has been beaten, terrorized, or shot for their money, or anyone who has been rejected or discriminated against because of their race, religion, or nationality. More often than not, such victims will tell you they had similar feelings towards their assailants.

Max: I don't doubt what you say, Siddhartha.

Siddhartha: And is it not the belief that you have been *wronged* that gives rise to your indignation?

Max: That is true. It is hard not to feel that way when you have been seriously harmed or disregarded.

Siddhartha: Indeed. I discovered during the years I worked in the prison that even the most hardened criminal has deep feelings of indignation when completely disregarded by others. Indeed, prisoners are passionately indignant whenever *they* are the victims. You will find no greater righteousness than in such criminals when another has wronged *them*. In point of fact, you will find that there is but one class of individuals that are an exception to this general rule.

Max: And who are they?

Siddhartha: Those who have the most gentle, most loving, and most forgiving natures of all. It takes the most noble souls of all to really be able to say, "Forgive them, for they know not what they do," and to really mean it and feel it with their whole being. I recall a striking example of this. A young man of thirty had been senselessly shot by a youngster of only sixteen, and was consequently paralyzed. I saw the victim being interviewed, and everything in his bearing and manner told me he meant it when he stated that he bore neither hatred nor malice for the youngster. His concern was for a world where such a thing could happen. But let us note that even such exceptions prove the rule. For even in such cases, although the victim bears no anger towards the assailant, the victim still understands that what was done to him was morally wrong. For those who have such gentle natures would be the last to say that people ought to treat one another as they have been treated.

Max: That is very true, Siddhartha. I know the young man of whom you speak, and I was astounded by his completely forgiving nature.

Siddhartha: Now let me ask you this, Max. Does it matter who it is that violates you, if they are totally disregarding of you and completely indifferent to your happiness, honor, and autonomy?

Max: I must confess it does not. When it is perfectly clear that the assailant is totally disregarding of me as a human being, I feel the very same indignation. I would only qualify this by adding that, were it to be a friend or intimate, I would only feel worse and more indignant, for that would reveal him to have been a false friend, which would only add to the violence of his disregard for me.

Siddhartha: Yes, I can see it would add to the treachery of the act if he had pretended to be your friend as well. But the point is that you would feel indignant no matter who performed the act.

Max: That is true.

Siddhartha: Moreover, it is the fact that what he does is inconsistent with your self-love, that gives rise to such feelings. For had he been mindful of your self-love, had he been mindful of the fact that your happiness, autonomy, honor, self-acceptance, and self-appreciation mean as much to you as his to himself, you would not have felt so wronged and therefore so indignant. Is that not so?

Max: I cannot deny what you say.

Siddhartha: Well, can you see, then, Max, how we humans all have a natural tendency to live by a double set of standards?

Max: A double set of standards?

Siddhartha: Yes. There is the set of moral standards we tend to live by as *victims,* and then there is the set we live by as *agents.* When we judge the rightness or wrongness of what others do to us, we apply the standard of self-love; if they do something that is inconsistent with our self-love, we tend to condemn it as wrong. Hence, our natural, rational standard as victims is the standard of love; we hold that *all* others ought to treat us in ways consistent with the love we ideally bear for ourselves. So as *victims,* we are all naturally inclined to be *absolutists.* That is, when it comes to what is done to us we are naturally inclined to judge anything anyone does to us by one and the same standard—the standard of love. And this is true of the criminal no less than of you and me. But when we are considering what we do to others—*the agent's perspective*—due to the pull of the subjective point of view, we are inclined to apply the most lenient standards we can get by with. As *agents* we are inclined to permit ourselves all sorts of liberties that, from a victim's point of view, we would condemn as morally wrong. Do you now see what I mean when I speak of our natural tendency towards a double set of standards?

Max: I do indeed. And I think that any honest person will own up to what you say.

S: we tend to be hypocritical, & to insist on the moral point of view only / esp. when we are victims

This seems like a repetition of S's earlier arg. that rationality demands that we act morally & self-love

Siddhartha: Then note that all that the Golden Rule is telling us to do is to apply the very same standard of love when we do things that affect others that we apply when others do things that affect us. In short, the Golden Rule is telling us to have the very same regard for everyone else's self-love that we, in fact, demand *everyone* else have for our own self-love. In doing so the Golden Rule is instructing us to put an end to our natural tendency to apply a double set of standards. From the purely subjective perspective, such a double set of standards is entirely appealing and entirely rational. But from the objective perspective, it is obvious that such double-dealing arises out of selfish motives. Such double-dealing is completely unworthy and so, from an objective perspective, completely irrational. Yet out of a rational self-love, we would always place the objective perspective above the subjective perspective. Hence, out of rational self-love, we would always follow the Golden Rule.

Max: As I see it, your argument here rests upon two assumptions: On the one hand, you have argued that there is a universal tendency, out of rational self-love, to feel and really believe we are wronged whenever anyone deliberately and totally disregards us and acts in a way that is seriously inconsistent with our own self-love. On the other hand, you are assuming that since this is the standard we, in fact, apply as victims, then if our lives are to have worth from the objective perspective, we must apply those very same standards to ourselves as agents. Is that right?

Siddhartha: That is right.

Max: Granted these conclusions and Homer's contention that it is rational to place the objective above the subjective view, I can see how you can conclude that following the Golden Rule is the only rational way to live. Nor can I deny that you have not made a strong case for your two assumptions. Nonetheless, Siddhartha, we are still a long way from anything I would want to call science. Nor am I certain science can explain or make sense out of all of this. Let us grant for the sake of argument that you have adequately refuted Dilemma's claim that science favors relativism over absolutism. What do you say to the *moral skeptic* who says: "Science or nothing. What you have shown me is not science, Siddhartha, but is, at best, a kind of common sense or folk psychology. Hence, you have shown me nothing''?

Siddhartha: You mean, I take it, that I have done nothing that would impress a certain kind of skeptic. Having heard my arguments, he will stick with his skepticism because he wants science or nothing. Is that it?

Max: That's it exactly. The moral skeptic would doubt your assumptions, since they have not been established scientifically. Hence, he would deny that you or anyone else has any knowledge of the things of which you speak. How would you reply to such a skeptic?

Siddhartha: How indeed? That is a good question. But before I try to answer it, I would like to draw a distinction.

Max: And what might that be?

Siddhartha: A distinction between knowledge and rational presumption. As a rule, if it is more rational to believe something than to withhold belief *purely on the evidence alone,* then if what is believed is true, the believer has a *knowledge* of that thing. What I am calling a rational presumption has weaker conditions than knowledge does. First of all, something may be a rational presumption even if it turns out to be false, and this is not the case with knowledge. Second, something may be a rational presumption even though it is not more rational to believe it than not to believe it on the evidence alone. A rational presumption, then, may be defined as follows: Something is a *rational presumption* just in case, *on the basis of the evidence along with the associated consequences,* it is more rational to believe it than not to believe it.

Max: I see. Could you give us an example of a rational presumption?

Siddhartha: Suppose the four of us were lost at sea in a small lifeboat and we had not the least notion of how far we were from land or what our chances of survival were. As far as the evidence alone goes, we could not say it was more rational to believe we had a chance of surviving than to have no such belief. Yet it would be equally true to say that the evidence alone did not make it more reasonable to withhold belief either. Hence we could not be said to *know* either that we could survive or that we could not survive. Now I believe it is quite clear that someone in such circumstances who believes survival is possible has an enormously greater chance of surviving than someone who entirely lacks such a belief. Hence, in such circumstances, it would be clearly more reasonable to assume that survival is possible then to be unwilling to make such an assumption. And this would be so even if, as it turned out, our situation was such that survival was indeed not possible. For as we noted, we could have no way of knowing such a thing. Hence, our belief that we could survive in such a situation would be an example of a *rational presumption,* but not of knowledge.

Max: And just how do you plan to use this distinction in answering the moral skeptic?

Siddhartha: I propose to answer the skeptic by agreeing with some of the things he says, while disagreeing with others. First of all, I deny that there are no ethical truths that are known. Consider the ethical truth that it is morally wrong to slowly torture a baby to death just for the fun of it. There is no society and no sane person who would deny the truth or at least the rightness of such a moral precept. I say that there is sufficient evidence to make it more reasonable to believe than not to believe that precept on the evidence alone. If so, then that would be an example of ethical knowledge. So first of all I reject the skeptic's blanket statement that there is no moral knowledge at all.

Max: I cannot deny that I am sympathetic with what you say so far. But though you can point to some ethical precepts about which there is virtually universal agreement, as we have all of us noted, there are significant areas of disagreement as well. What about that?

Siddhartha: That brings me to the Golden Rule. I do not claim to *know* that the Golden Rule is the supreme principle of all morality. However, I do say it is a *rational presumption* on my part to believe in that principle.

Max: I am afraid I still can't really agree with you on that, though I must admit that your arguments have been sufficiently compelling that I can see how a very intelligent and very reasonable person such as yourself has come to believe it is a rational presumption on your part. For my part, I still think the rational presumption is ethical relativism. Be that as it may, I would still like to ask you this: Wouldn't you rather say that you *know* that the Golden Rule is the supreme principle of all morality and not simply that it is a rational presumption of yours?

Siddhartha: There is no denying I would like to be able to say I know it and not simply that I rationally presume it to be the one true morality. But given the definition of knowledge I have given above, I don't think I can say this. For I must admit that, at present, the evidence alone is not sufficiently strong to enable me to say that it is unreasonable to deny that the Golden Rule is the single, true principle of morality. Only the evidence, along with the associated consequences, makes such a denial irrational, in my opinion. At the same time, there is always the future. I don't say that the Golden Rule will come to be sufficiently supported by the evidence to constitute knowledge in the future, but I would not rule out such a possibility either. So here is another point on which I and the skeptic disagree, for I allow for the possibility of such ethical knowledge in the future, while the moral skeptic does not. Moreover, I believe it is just as irrational for the moral skeptic to deny such a possibility as it would be for someone in the lifeboat situation to deny the possibility that they can be saved. Thus, although I agree with the moral skeptic that we currently have no *knowledge* of the ultimate principles of ethics, the areas where I disagree are quite significant indeed. And where we disagree, I further hold that it is my presumptions and not those of the moral skeptic that are rational.

S's response to moral skepticism is that, even if there isn't moral knowledge (in fact there is), moral principles can be supported as rational presumptions *realism has better consequences than moral skepticism*

Max: In saying that the rational presumption is in your favor and not that of the moral skeptic, I take it, it is more the consequences than the evidence you have in mind.

Siddhartha: I have both in mind. But you are right that the consequences are a very important factor. For I believe that the consequences of taking moral skepticism completely seriously would be disastrous.

Max: I must say that I am quite sympathetic with your point concerning the disastrous consequences of assuming the moral skeptic's position. For in the end I think it leads to nihilism and confusion and allows no significant role for reason to play in our practical, ethical choices. However, unlike you, I see relativism and not absolutism as the reasonable alternative. It is because of the variation in ethical norms that the moral skeptic can get his foot in the door in the first place. Moral relativism turns him abruptly back into the cold again, however, by cheerfully conceding that point while quickly adding that what is truly morally right and wrong itself varies, so that it is scarcely surprising that people's moral norms vary. In any case, there is still a considerable distance between our respective positions. However, now that I understand more clearly what we both agree and disagree on regarding these fundamental questions, I am content to turn you over to Homer. There is much more I would like to question you about, but I have taken a lion's share of your time already.

Siddhartha: I am certain we have much more to discuss and to learn from one another, Max. But I agree with you that time is going by, and I see that Homer is ready with a fresh batch of new questions for me. Please ask away, Homer.

M agrees that moral skepticism is wrong. However it can be undercut by relativism, w/o resorting to absolutism

Wrongness of moral skepticism ↛ absolutism

Part VI

Homer's Reservations about Absolutism

Homer: You have made out an impressive case for the principle of love, Siddhartha. You may convert me yet. However, I still have some serious misgivings that I would like to address.

Siddhartha: And what might these be?

Homer: As you yourself have just pointed out, it is reasonable to consider the consequences and not simply the evidence associated with the beliefs we are discussing.

Siddhartha: That is quite true.

Homer: Now, in many ways I think that believing in the Golden Rule can only have good effects upon the believer's life and conduct. However, it is one thing to believe in the Golden Rule *for yourself,* Siddhartha, and another to believe that it is the single, true moral principle *for everyone.* For this latter belief seems to carry a danger with it, not attaching to the former. The danger I speak of is the danger of intolerance. One of the things that a lot of us find attractive about relativism is that we believe that it breeds humility and tolerance and makes it possible for people having different moral orientations to accept and get along with each other. My central question to you then is this:

absolutism may breed intolerance

What can you as an absolutist do to avoid moral arrogance and moral intolerance?

Siddhartha: You have indeed identified an important problem in moral life, Homer, and we must do our best to examine it with great care. But let us begin by making some observations on the topic of intolerance. First of all, being a relativist does not automatically protect you from either moral arrogance or moral intolerance. For example, let us not forget that Benito Mussolini, who was a Fascist and who was extremely arrogant and intolerant, was a self-professed moral relativist. Indeed, he saw Fascism and moral relativism as mutually supporting doctrines.

Homer: Your point is very well taken, Siddhartha. However, it is possible to both accept the principle of moral humility and moral tolerance for yourself, and at the same time be a relativist. And that combination seems the best protection against moral arrogance and moral intolerance I can think of.

Siddhartha: Whether or not that combination is the best protection against arrogance and intolerance is something we should examine. What, for example, would you do if you saw another, right within your own society, practicing intolerance? How far would your principles tell you to go if, for example, you saw Fascism on the rise in the United States? To what extent would you tolerate such a thing?

Homer: I would be deeply troubled by such a spectacle. That is certain. Yet I would have to permit the Fascists free speech, for the elimination of free speech is more of a risk to democracy than mere talk of Fascism is. However, I would oppose the *practice* of Fascism with my life if need be.

Siddhartha: Knowing what a brave and noble soul you are, Homer, I do not doubt what you say for a moment. But tell me upon what grounds would you oppose Fascism? Would you describe these as moral grounds?

Homer: I would.

Siddhartha: And what would you say of those advocating Fascism? Can they not also claim to promote Fascism on the grounds that, from their point of view, Fascism as a basis for conduct is morally right?

Homer: I would have to admit that that is so.

Siddhartha: Indeed, you could not, as a good relativist, say that your moral perspective is, in any *moral* sense, superior to theirs. Isn't that true?

Homer: It is. But I can say that mine is as valid as theirs. Moreover, since it is the one I am committed to, I can, with consistency, support mine by opposing theirs.

Siddhartha: Let us grant that you can consistently and coherently defend such a position. There is no place for a rational, moral dialogue between you and the Fascist, for, granted your relativist position, there simply is no possibility of rationally demonstrating the superiority of your moral position over his on any moral grounds. For there are no neutral *moral* grounds to stand on outside of your respective moral views.

Homer: I am not happy about these consequences of relativism, but I agree that I cannot escape them.

Siddhartha: Then let us note that from the start this places some rather serious limits upon the role that we can even hope reason might play in moral life. When serious clashes arise between basic moral principles, there is no way of appealing to reason—unless you can show your opponent, the Fascist for instance, that his principles are inconsistent with one another or with his society's various interests. Failing to do that, your only solution is to appeal to mutual selfish interests or to take up arms against one another. Gandhi's passive resistance and the like are useless, for such approaches can only work by means of their *moral force.* And on your assumption of relativism, there is no moral force to be applied in case of such clashes.

Reason, the moral force of arg—, can have no role to play if relativism is true / accepted

Homer: I accept your claim that all of this is a consequence of relativism. But I doubt that you can get any further in trying to reason with a Fascist than we relativists. The Fascist will laugh at you no less than at us, for he despises reason except as it serves his Fascist aspirations. *good reply!*

Siddhartha: Perhaps. Perhaps not. There is still a difference. If reason fails in my case, it fails for *psychological* reasons: It is confronting a fanatic. But in the case of relativism, it must fail no matter who the opponent is for it fails for *philosophical* reasons: You as a relativist can't even make the attempt. You must despair before you even try. It is a matter of policy for any good relativist not to look for any neutral moral grounds. The relativist on both sides must assume there is no sense in which one moral system is *morally* superior to the other. Gandhi's notion of passive resistance, what he called soul force and what I call moral force, assumes a universal, moral law—the law of love, as Gandhi referred to it. According to the relativist such a practice could only work for disputes between persons already sharing the same essential, moral outlook. I believe, however, that Gandhi's soul force was an important experiment with profound implications for our present-day world. You will find in human history few more tolerant or humble persons than Gandhi. Yet he was an unflinching absolutist when it came to the law of love or the Golden Rule. I believe, in fact, Homer, that you will not find a sounder basis for genuine humility and tolerance than the law of love.

Homer: I am not as sure about that as you, Siddhartha. For we must not forget the many horrible, intolerant things people have done throughout history in the name of a love ethic. From the imperialism of the Europeans to the persecution of nonbelievers, the record is shameful.

Siddhartha: That is entirely true. But let us note that there were certain religious doctrines as well as various economic and political motives that were at work in such cases. Even more important, to do something in the name of love is one thing, to truly be loving is an entirely different thing. For in any of the

Does the 'love ethic' have good consequences?

cases you have in mind, is there a single one that is consistent with the law of love?

Homer: I suppose not.

Siddhartha: Then you suppose rightly, for it could scarcely be the case that someone can act in a way that is consistent with everyone's self-love and yet be arrogant and intolerant. In fact, I ask you this: Can you think of a single example of anyone doing anything you would call immoral while at the same time acting in a way that is consistent with *everyone's* rational self-love?

Homer: I must admit that nothing comes to mind.

Siddhartha: Then how could you find a sounder basis for the principles of humility and tolerance than the law of love itself? For what could tell you better just how far to go and in what way you should act in exercising those lesser principles than the law of love itself?

Homer: I can think of none at the moment, Siddhartha. And yet I am still beset with gnawing doubts. For example, it seems as if, granted the law of love is the supreme principle of ethics, the rich diversity of cultures that we have today is unlawful, and there is really only a single monolithic culture we all ought to be moving toward. And such a notion of a single, monolithic world culture seems a subtle, but very real and very dangerous form of intolerance to me.

Siddhartha: What you describe, the invalidation of the many rich cultures that exist today, would indeed be a genuine and dangerous form of intolerance. But that very sort of cultural violence is forbidden, not required by the Golden Rule. There is no doubt that *reform* in every culture would be required by the law of love, but not its *abolition*. For don't forget that if we are to act in ways that are consistent with everyone's self-love, then we must respect all persons' autonomy and self-government, and we must moreover accept and appreciate them in their otherness, which is to say in their differences.

Homer: But how can differences in moral norms and moral practices be acceptable, if there is but one, true morality?

Siddhartha: From the vantage point of an ethic of love, moral norms or rules are best thought of as rules of thumb or general specifications of actions that will usually fulfill the moral law by being consistent with everyone's self-love. As such they are imperfect: Lying, for example, as a rule is not consistent with everyone's rational self-love. So as a rule honesty is required by the law of love. But there are exceptions. For example, giving an honest answer about the location of a gun to an insane man intent on killing someone would not be a loving act. Moral norms admit of a certain leeway, moreover: One may contribute to those who are needy in very different ways, according to one's own talents, interests, and resources. Furthermore, in different cultures people have different needs. For example, a car might well be said to be a necessity for a salesman who covers a rural route in today's world, but not ninety years ago when very few people had cars. Nor does the law of love in any way directly concern itself with that aspect of religious life that has to do with people's relationship to God. To the contrary, a respect for people's autonomy forbids such interference. I believe, in general, that the more you think on the matter, Homer, the more you will agree with me that there simply is no reason to expect that adherence to the law of love would do anything but preserve the variety and integrity of the various cultures and subcultures around the world. Love is variety's best ally.

Homer: Perhaps you are right, Siddhartha. All the same, what is to prevent me from arguing that I may adopt the law of love *for myself*, and mine, without assuming absolutism, that is, without assuming that those who live according to opposing moral principles are necessarily morally wrong? Am I not in danger of a certain subtle moral arrogance in making such an assumption? Do I not do a certain violence to their self-esteem by insisting upon my morality as the one, true morality?

Siddhartha: Were I to judge *them* morally, you are perfectly right. For that would be inconsistent with practicing the law of

love. But my judgment is not about them at all, but about the
status of the principle of love itself—that it is universally valid
for everyone and in that sense absolute. Logically, a commit-
ment to the universal rightness of the law of love does entail that
any act, rule, or principle that is inconsistent with someone's
rational self-love is indeed wrong, but it does not entail any
judgment about the *ultimate* moral worth of persons performing
such acts or living by such rules or principles. This is not for us
to judge, for indeed to do so would be inconsistent with that
person's rational self-love and so, paradoxically, with the law of
love itself.

Homer: Still, why is it important to insist that love is the
supreme law of all ethics, *for everyone?*

Siddhartha: First of all, I have already argued that it is rational
for *anyone,* and not simply for me, to presume that the Golden
Rule is the supreme principle of all morality. If you find my
arguments in support of that contention compelling, then you
already have sufficient grounds for believing in the absoluteness
of the law of love. There are, moreover, two additional reasons
for insisting that the Golden Rule is absolute. One is that the
absoluteness of the Golden Rule is a logical, conceptual requirement; the other is that it is a practical, substantive requirement.
Consider the logical requirement first. Suppose you are in a
position to prevent one person, call him Jones, from brutally
murdering another, Smith. And let us further suppose that you
are not in your own country, but in Jones's country, and that,
in Jones's country, it is perfectly legal and moral for Jones to
murder Smith in this way, since Smith is Jones's slave, and
slaves are regarded as property to be used as the owner wishes.
Now you could *easily* save Smith, by taking him into your car
and racing him to the border of another country only a quarter
of a mile away at a crossing where you happen to know there
are no guards to stop you. What would you say is required of
you in this situation according to the Golden Rule?

Homer: Very clearly the Golden Rule requires me to save
Smith's life, as I would want done for me in that same situation.

Saving Smith would be consistent with my own self-love and Smith's as well. So that is the thing I must do in this situation.

Siddhartha: Good so far. But now what about Jones? Are you acting in a way that is consistent with Jones's self-love?

Homer: But Jones is responsible for the situation. I don't need to consider him.

Siddhartha: Not so. The Golden Rule requires you to consider everyone's self-love and to do what is consistent with everyone's self-love. So you can't just ignore Jones and treat him as a nonperson simply because he is responsible for the situation. Therefore, we must think through our action in terms of Jones's self-love as well.

Homer: You are right, Siddhartha. But how shall we do this?

Siddhartha: Let's do it from two perspectives, first from an absolutist perspective and then from a relativist perspective, and see what the difference is.

Homer: That sounds fine to me.

Siddhartha: If we assume that the law of love is the supreme principle of all morality for everyone, we assume that everyone is morally bound by it, then we may reason as follows: What Jones is about to do is morally wrong *for Jones* and not simply for us, or from our perspective. Therefore, Jones is placing the subjective perspective above the objective perspective—his own happiness and well-being above the moral law—and so acting irrationally and in a way that is inconsistent with his own self-love. Now it is not our place to interfere with Jones's honor or morality, for the law of love says we must respect his autonomy. However, we do have a duty to Smith to save his life and to protect Smith's autonomy. Hence, since Jones is exercising his autonomy in a way that unlawfully interferes with the autonomy, life, and well-being of Smith, it is not contrary to Jones's rational self-love for us to prevent Jones from carrying out his act. As absolutists we can reason this way just because Jones is bound

[handwritten annotation: Relativism prevents interference with moral action; but such interference is required by any morality such as the love ethic. So relativism isn't a moral position.]

by the very same law of love as we are, whether he acknowl-
edges that fact or not.

Homer: Ah, I see. And you want to say that a similar line of
argument is not possible, if we are relativist. Is that it?

Siddhartha: Yes. For consider this same problem from a relativist perspective. Suppose you are a relativist who regards the law
of love as the supreme principle of morality *for you,* and for
those who accept it as such, *but not for everyone.* In particular,
you agree that there is no neutral, transcultural grounds or
standpoint from which you can say your law of love is in any
way morally superior to Jones's slave-owner morality. But if
that is the case, then in this situation you would be *imposing*
your morality upon Jones against his will, and so interfering
with his autonomy and his self-love. And this, your own principle of love forbids you to do. Nor can you argue that Jones is
really the one whose actions are inconsistent with his own self-
love and violative of *his* own moral law, for this is not the case.
Jones's moral law is the slave-owner's morality, and that permits
him to do what you are preventing him from doing. So if you are
a relativist and trying to follow the Golden Rule, you will get
into the following double bind: Either you will save Smith and
so act in a way that is consistent with Smith's self-love but not
consistent with Jones's self-love, or you will not save Smith and
so do what is consistent with Jones's self-love but not with
Smith's. In short, it is impossible to do what is consistent with
everyone's self-love if you assume the Golden Rule is only valid
for some, but not for others. Absolutism is therefore inherent in
the law of love: Being a relativist and a follower of the love ethic
is an incoherent notion.

Homer: I see that you are right in what you say, Siddhartha.
And by itself that suffices to explain why you can't accept the
love ethic and still remain a relativist. But you said there was a
second, practical, consideration to take note of as well. I would
be interested to hear what that is.

Siddhartha: It is my belief that more than ever, the world is in
need of moral clarity, and that an ethic of love alone has the
power to provide the world with this much-needed clarity.

Ends with a rather Apocalyptic vision of an urgent need for "moral clarity" (in light of impending disaster), which only an ethic of love can provide

104   Part VI

Homer: Why do you say that the need for moral clarity is greater than ever?

Siddhartha: Because, as I see it, the human race is heading for a crisis of a magnitude comparable to the one that destroyed the dinosaur. Only, our crisis is entirely of our own making and largely within our power to manage, if only we will collectively choose to do so.

Homer: I take it you are referring to the current stock of nuclear weapons that threaten the survival of the human race?

Siddhartha: I am referring to that, but I am referring to other problems technology has produced for us as well, such as the destruction of the environment, the population explosion, and the turbulence of the world economy. These and many other offspring of modern technology impose upon the contemporary world an urgency and need for cooperation among people of diverse cultural orientations and outlooks such as is unprecedented in the entire history of the world. Nor will this need cease with the solving of the above-mentioned problems, for with their solutions there will forever be new problems of a similar magnitude to take their place. That is the price we must pay for our technology, for every advance in technology shrinks the world, magnifies our powers, and provides us with new dangers and new ways of destroying ourselves if we so choose. It is this tendency of technology to be a double-edged sword that I refer to when I speak of the unprecedented need for moral clarity. For unless we as a world can be clear about our moral priorities and see them with a single pair of ethical eyes, as it were, we will never achieve the necessary consensus and cooperation needed to manage these problems sanely and wisely.

Homer: And you believe that an ethic of love alone can provide us with this necessary common moral vision. Is that it?

Siddhartha: It is indeed. In my opinion there is no other ethical principle upon which there lies the hope of such a unified vision. For the law of love alone respects each and every person's self-love with an equal regard—a condition I hold is necessary in order for any moral principle to win universal, rational assent.

Homer: I see.

Siddhartha: So you see, Homer, this is another reason why it is necessary to regard the law of love as absolute. For upon that assumption rests the hope that we can solve the problems that face us, enormous as they are. If I am right in thinking that our best hope for safely navigating the stormy seas technology has brought us to is an ethic of love, then one could scarcely ask for a stronger reason for making the Golden Rule the universal sextant for this spaceship we call earth. I can scarcely think of anything that would make my presumption in favor of the absoluteness of the love ethic any more rational than that.

Homer: Well said, Siddhartha. For it is indeed hard to imagine a stronger consideration than the fate of the entire race. You have indeed given me some very powerful additional reasons to seriously consider the Golden Rule. For the moment, however, I think it is time to draw our discussion to a close, if the rest of you agree. I think I am a bit dizzy from it all. But be assured, Siddhartha, it is a dizziness that is quite pleasant and that will bring with it a new clarity in the days to come.

Suggested Readings

Aristotle. *Nicomachean Ethics,* found in *Introduction to Aristotle,* edited by Richard McKeon. New York: The Modern Library, 1947.

Augustine, St. *The City of God.* Garden City, N.Y.: Doubleday & Company, Inc., 1958.

Baier, K. *The Moral Point of View.* Ithaca, N.Y.: Cornell University Press, 1958.

Benedict, Ruth. *Patterns of Culture.* Boston: Houghton Mifflin, 1934.

Buber, Martin. *I and Thou.* New York: Charles Scribner & Sons, 1958.

Butler, Joseph. *Fifteen Sermons Upon Human Nature,* 1726.

Frankena, William. *Ethics.* Englewood Cliffs, N.J.: Prentice-Hall, 1973.

Hare, R. M. *The Language of Morals.* New York: Oxford University Press, 1964.

Harman, Gilbert. *The Nature of Morality: An Introduction to Ethics.* New York: Oxford University Press, 1977.

Herskovits, Melville J. *Cultural Relativism.* New York: Random House, 1973.

Hobbes, Thomas. *Leviathan,* edited by M. Oakeshott. New York: Oxford University Press, 1945.

Hocutt, Max. *First Philosophy: An Introduction to Philosophical Issues.* Malabar, Fla.: Robert E. Krieger Publishing Company, 1980.

Hospers, John. *Human Conduct.* New York: Harcourt, Brace & World, 1961.

Hume, David. *An Enquiry Concerning the Principles of Morals.* Cambridge, Mass.: Hackett Publishing Company, 1983.

Kane, R. *Free Will and Value.* Albany: State University of New York Press, 1985.

Kant, Immanuel. *The Groundwork of the Metaphysics of Morals,* edited and translated by H. J. Paton. New York: Harper Torchbooks, 1964.

Kierkegaard, Soren. *Works of Love.* New York: Harper Torchbooks, 1962.

Ladd, John, editor. *Ethical Relativism.* Belmont, Calif.: Wadsworth Books, 1973.

MacIver, R. M. "The Deep Beauty of the Golden Rule," in *Moral Principles of Action,* edited by Ruth Nanda Anshen. New York: Harper & Row.

Midgley, Mary. *Heart and Mind.* New York: St. Martin's Press, 1981.

Mill, John Stuart. *Utilitarianism.* New York: Liberal Arts Press, 1957.

Moore, G. E. *Ethics.* New York: Oxford University Press, 1965.

――――. *Principia Ethica.* Cambridge, England: Cambridge University Press, 1903.

Nietzsche, Friedrich. *Beyond Good and Evil.* Chicago: Henry Regnery Company, 1955.

Plato. *Republic,* editor and translator F. M. Cornford. Fair Lawn, N.J.: Oxford University Press, 1945.

Rawls, John. *A Theory of Justice.* Cambridge, Mass.: Harvard University Press, 1971.

Skinner, B. F. *Beyond Freedom and Dignity.* New York: Vintage, 1977.

――――. *Walden Two.* New York: Macmillan, 1962.

Stace, W. T. *The Concept of Morals.* New York: Macmillan Paperbacks, 1962.

Stevenson, Charles L. *Facts and Values.* New Haven: Yale University Press, 1964.

Taylor, Richard. *Good and Evil.* Buffalo: Prometheus Press, 1970.

Warnock, Mary. *Ethics Since 1900.* New York: Oxford University Press, 1960.

Westermarck, Edward A. *Ethical Relativity*. New York: Harcourt, 1932.

Wong, David. *Moral Relativity*. Los Angeles: University of California Press, 1984.